# TO HAVE
# AND
# TO HOLD

**John-Michael Hendrix**

To Rick Jewell,
Best wishes!
Your Friend,
John Michael

Packaged by WinePress Publishing, PO Box 1406, Mukilteo, WA 98275. The views expressed or implied in this work do not necessarily reflect those of WinePress Publishing. Ultimate design, content, and editorial accuracy of this work is the responsibility of the author(s).

ISBN 1-57921-103-8
Library of Congress Catalog Card Number: 98-60197

This is for Patti. Without your love there would never have been a book to be written.

This book is dedicated

To my mother, June Hendrix, who taught me the meaning of truth and perseverance.

To Patti's parents, Kingsley and Ruth Gingell, who guided her to integrity and kindness for others and raised her to their own high ideals.

To our daughters Heather, Heidi, and Hollyann who are the result of the love between their mother and me.

To Hazel Bartam Donnelly. In remembrance of all the young lives you have touched.

# Contents

# Preface

During the war in Vietnam, I served three tours of duty in combat as an infantry officer and helicopter pilot. While a member of a special volunteer unit, many of my experiences in Vietnam were unusual. By age twenty-two, I was a decorated "old timer" with four Distinguished Flying Crosses and had been shot down on seven occasions. In the midst of my last tour, I met and married, in Vietnam, a US Army nurse. We are still happily married twenty-eight years later.

In writing of my experiences, I have tried to be more than just realistic and accurate on the combat scenes. I have written also on the daily life and subtle humor of the men and women who served and did more than only fight. I'll note to you here that what I have written in the manuscript provided is reality. The events occurred. Nothing is made up.

My end desire was to complete a book describing my combat experiences with special emphasis on the relationship my wife and I had, not only to each other, but to those around us whose lives touched ours.

I hope you will enjoy reading what I have written.

Regards,

JOHN-MICHAEL HENDRIX

# Foreword

Anyone who goes to war comes back with a story to tell. Unfortunately, few people write it down. Old newspapers, film archives, and historians can tell who won the battles and a little of how it looked, but what gets lost is what happened to individual soldiers. The Vietnam War was fought by nineteen-year-old boys, far from home and far from what they knew and understood. More happened to them than we will ever know.

And almost as hurtful to them as anything that happened in the war, they returned anonymously to the States with no thanks or recognition. Amid a national debate over the fighting in Vietnam, there were no parades for the soldiers who came home.

Twenty-eight years after leaving Vietnam, John-Michael Hendrix, now living in Granite Falls, Washington, wrote a book to tell his children what he did in Vietnam and how he met their mother. It is a war story and a love story simply told.

Hendrix was the pilot of an observation helicopter. He spent his war years flying at low level looking for enemy troops. He also met, courted, and married a surgical nurse, Patti Gingell, from Euclid, Ohio. While back at home young men drove their girlfriends around in Detroit's muscle cars, Hendrix picked up his date in a helicopter fixed with a minigun.

I met John and Patti in the fall of 1997 after hearing about his book and how it was received by the kids in Debra Howell's class at Monte Cristo Elementary School in Granite Falls, WA. They were fascinated in particular with a daring pilot known as "Weird Bob". They begged Hendrix to find his old friend. That's about the time Producer Peter Imber and I went to Granite Falls to do a story for ABC News about John, Weird Bob, and the children of Debra Howell's class.

This book, *To Have and to Hold,* ends when Hendrix is wounded and leaves the war. When you finish reading, put the book down and think for a moment about a little town in the woods of Washington State where you can see from one end of Main Street to the other.

It is Veterans Day, nearly thirty years after the war, and the children of Debra Howell's class have organized a welcome home for "Weird Bob" to a town where he never lived and never even visited before this day. The street is lined with thousands of people as veterans from three wars march. In the midst, waving from a convertible, surrounded by children is Bob Donnelly—"Weird Bob". In the reviewing stand, proudly watching this welcome home, are John and Patti Hendrix.

It all happened because John Hendrix wrote his war story.

Brian Rooney
ABC News Correspondent
Los Angeles, February 1998

# Chapter 1

August 1970

Until a few days ago, Fire Support Base Ripcord had been just a brown spot on a high hill surrounded by sandbags in an otherwise green jungle. Until a few days ago, we had flown low over Ripcord in our helicopters en route to our operations area and, smiling, waved enthusiastically to the forsaken troops stuck there. Until a few days ago, they had waved back.

Then, after our day's missions were complete, we would fly to base, be served almost normal food, have a drink at the officers' club, sleep on a soft dry mattress with sheets and usually forget that Ripcord existed.

Today, we still flew low over Ripcord—the lower, the faster, the less likely you were to be a target. Teeth clenched and grinding, sweaty palms wrapped around the cyclic control, fingers no longer flashing a "V" sign out of the door.

Now our fingers were on the gun buttons and ready to kill. Ripcord was not surrounded by just sandbags anymore. It was surrounded by thousands of North Vietnamese soldiers.

There was no waving. There was no smiling. We would never again forget Ripcord.

Ripcord was one of many small hilltop positions. Not unlike the spokes of a wheel, they centered around a main hub and provided support and strength to it. The hub was the city of Hue. Camp Eagle, combat home of the 101st Airborne, was also there.

The hilltop posts served as positions from which patrols could be sent out to test enemy strength or their activity. They could also provide artillery support to small scale operations into what was considered enemy held territory.

The problem with these firebases was that they were difficult to protect from the main base under certain conditions such as bad weather. We were engaged in a helicopter war. If the helicopters were grounded, their support couldn't be given to those on the outskirts of civilization. There were few if any roads.

Even with our support, a trooper's life on one of these hills was miserable. Without it, the trooper resembled a defenseless chick in a pen with a hole in it, no mother hen and a weasel inside. He could move, run, or hide underground on what little acreage the hilltop had, but without roads leading in or out, he couldn't escape if overwhelmed.

There was one way in, one way out: helicopter. Food, people, ammunition, dead, wounded, everything. Only by helicopter.

This isolation is what doomed Ripcord. The weather was bad. Ripcord was vulnerable, and the enemy knew it.

For a week we scout pilots—whose job it was to seek out the enemy by following their activity, observing tracks left on the trails by troop movement or by being shot at—had not been able to fly. The bad weather became one of our continual nightmares.

A nightmare for the pilots, a living hell for guys on Ripcord. The weasel was sniffing, the mother hen was away and the chicks could not escape.

The enemy attacked. We could not help. We could only wait.

When the weather was finally clear enough to fly, the situation at Ripcord was horrible. By the third day, most of the low-level reconnaissance units, scouts from the original first reaction force, had lost at least one ship to enemy fire. A few guys from our troop were dead, a few more were wounded, and the rest of us were flat scared.

I was returning to a target area near Ripcord after rearming and fueling my ship from an earlier mission. Escorting me were my cover ships, two Cobra gun ships that protected me from enemy fire while I was doing my low-level recon job. We sometimes referred to them as Snakes.

The radio was going crazy with a multitude of messages. The command-in-control ship was giving orders to our troop carrier helicopters to prepare to evacuate the men left on Ripcord and to abandon the base.

The Cobras and I, along with any other helicopters with firepower on board, were to keep the enemy from overrunning the base until our troops could be cleared out.

The Air Force fighters were sucking oxygen at 20,000 feet and could hardly wait to rock and roll with napalm.

Those college boys truly loved to do business.

As we neared the target, we switched to our tactical frequency to monitor the scout who was down reconning and let him know that we were about ready to relieve him on station. Brian was the scout pilot working out. We were friends and had gotten to know each other reasonably well in the last few months. This was very unusual between two people with job functions that provided a very short life expectancy. Scout pilots were not famous for their longevity. Most did not get past the first name stage of a casual introduction.

Suddenly, Brian was screaming on the radio, "I'm hit! I'm hit!" Just as suddenly, there was silence. We were close enough that I could see his ship, puffing smoke, fly erratically out of the area. His cover ships, close behind, were firing rockets at flashes from enemy weapons.

The silence was broken by my cover leader calling me. "OK, Banshee 14, it's your turn. Are you ready?"

I checked my instrument panel and hoped for something to read too hot, high pressure . . . or maybe no pressure. Anything! No luck. No excuses. Everything was in the green.

"Stand by, One," I said and turned behind me to my gunner, Bill. Each scout ship carried two people. A pilot/observer and a gunner. The gunner's purpose was to provide supporting fire to protect my fanny if we were to draw enemy fire. I asked if he was ready. He patted his M-60 machine gun fondly and said, "Yeah, lieutenant, let's do it."

The child was certifiable. Anyone who would volunteer to ride in the back of a tiny helicopter, fly low-level through the jungle, skids almost touching the tree tops while tracking the enemy, was not mentally sound. When we were shot at, he would hang out of an open door of the ship on a strap and shoot back. Of course, there was nothing wrong with me. At least I was up front where the controls were.

In my most manly voice, trying to not squawk in a soprano, I called my lead, "In the green, let's play ball." There was an unwritten law that scout pilots had to sound cool on the radio no matter how bad the situation was.

I rolled out of the protection of the Cobras. I was to begin my recon over the trees just outside the wire perimeter of Ripcord. I saw the troop carrier aircraft approaching the hill in tight formation. Then the sky seemed to light up. Tracers! For every one you saw there were four non-tracer bullets speeding along invisible paths. "Taking fire!" I yelled into the radio. Bill was on the skids hanging by his monkey strap. Hot shell casings were flying everywhere and the Cobras were firing rockets behind me.

Out of my door I could see the enemy blanketing Ripcord's slopes, blowing the wire fence, and charging the hill. I madly pulled the trigger of my six-barreled mini-gun, sending 3,000 rounds a minute into the mass of advancing soldiers below. The noise was deafening.

An eternity later my "lead" radioed, "OK, little bird, our troops are out, the hill is clear. Come on up!" I did not argue.

When I got back to altitude, we all turned toward our main base and, with no reservations, tested just how much speed had been engineered into our aircraft. Lead called again and told me that we were done for the day. It was now the Air Force's turn to go in with their napalm and the big bombs.

Ripcord had changed owners and command wanted to make sure the price was a steep one. In my mind, it already had been.

On the way home I couldn't get Brian out of my mind. I had been shot down twice before, but I had never seen anyone else get hit as badly as he had been and still keep flying. It was a strange experience. I wondered if he was all right.

I keyed the radio, "Hello, lead, this is Banshee 14. Do you mind if I go to Phu Bai and see about 13? Fuel is good, no hits, and we are fine."

"Great," he said. "See you tonight at briefings. Let us know what you find out."

Phu Bai, just to our south, was home to the 85th Evacuation Hospital SMASH. (Semi-Mobile Army Surgical Hospital.)

I told Bill what was up and as usual he said, "Yeah, LT, let's do it."

As we approached, the aircraft controller at Phu Bai told me to stay clear of the hospital helicopter pad. It was busy. We landed on a ramp about forty yards away, near a fence where we would be out of the way.

I shut down the turbine engine and jumped out of the aircraft. I found myself face down in the dirt. My legs, earlier so tense, now were like rubber.

Trying to maintain some dignity, I collected myself and turned to Bill. "I'm going to go see if Brian made it here," I said. "I'll be back shortly."

Bill was happily changing barrels on his M-60 machine gun. Not long ago the barrel had been white hot. His oil rags were busily wiping dust away from little areas where metal parts met metal parts. "OK, lieutenant, see you later," he replied, while humming some new song he had heard on the local Armed Forces radio network.

As I walked away, I wondered about Bill. If there had been no war, which Federal Prison would he have inhabited? He loved this so-called lifestyle. In a way, this sort of life loved him. He did his job well and in doing so, helped keep me alive. Even though he was only nineteen years old, he was an old-timer here.

Nearing the hospital, I turned a corner around the fence and walked into a scene that even my worst dreams could not imagine. Wounded were everywhere. Heavy black plastic bags were scattered around. Body bags.

I hadn't left Ripcord behind me. The survivors were here before me and so were the dead.

I sidestepped stretchers. I was overwhelmed by the carnage. Doctors and nurses moved among the wounded with precision. I felt strange and out of place. My every step felt heavy. It was like seeing through someone else's eyes.

I had shot people before but had never been party to the consequences of such wounds or seen the suffering. One trooper asked for his mother. Other than that there was little sound. It was as if a heavy fog hung over this place, quenching any noise.

Quietly, carefully, I walked toward a set of double doors with a sign nailed above: Emergency Room. I thought that the whole landing area qualified for that.

People rushed by paying no attention to me. (Probably because I was standing, I thought.) "Excuse me, lieutenant, can I help you?" I saw lips move but heard nothing.

"Excuse me, but you are in the way. What is it that you want?" Then I heard and noticed that a nurse was talking to me.

She was beautiful. Green eyes. Blonde hair. She did not belong here. She should have been home or lying on a beach drenched in golden sunshine. Not here. Not now.

As I struggled to find my voice, I couldn't help feeling that she was someone special. I felt as if I had known her in another time, another place.

"Hi," I said. "Ah . . . I'm looking for Brian. A warrant officer . . . a pilot. Is he here?" Only after regaining my composure was I able to give her his last name and I.D. number.

"Let me get this straight," she shot back. "There's one hundred guys wounded. They are outside, inside, and everywhere in between. You want *one* fellow? Go stand over there out of the way. *Now!*"

And I did. Slowly I backed up until my heels touched an object behind me. Another body bag.

"Brian," I thought, "I hope you are alive so that I can tell you, personally, what you have put me through."

An hour passed.

"Excuse me, excuse me." (It was *that* nurse.) "I found your friend, lieutenant. He's in Quan Tri, thirty miles north. He's all right. His gunner flew the machine back. I spoke to his doctor on the open line and explained that you wanted to know his condition. They say he's doing well but not well enough to talk. You better go home."

I turned, without even saying thank you. Putting on my flight helmet, I started to walk away. Where had I known her?

I had spent the morning being shot at, gone searching unknown worlds for a friend, met a person that I couldn't get out of my mind, and now I was told, "Go home." While I struggled past the wounded, I remembered that I had another mission briefing to attend and tomorrow another mission. Always another mission.

Brian was all right. Goodbyes could wait. With each step something inside me told me I was wrong to go away, that I was leaving a part of me behind. With my helmet on I didn't hear the nurse calling, "Hey, what's your name? What's your unit?"

I found my ship and Bill. As I flew back to main base I felt a hollow spot in my stomach. It had been a long day.

A week passed. During that time I joined what was left of our reconnaissance unit in searching for a suddenly invisible enemy.

The gentlemen we had fought had not only overrun a firebase belonging to one of the best equipped units of the USA, but they had also overcome the additional problem of a reasonably good South Vietnamese Army unit being involved against them. And they had vanished. Over night, several thousand enemy troops were gone, taking with them our howitzers and other equipment left behind. It was amazing.

We pilots spoke very little among ourselves of this disappearing act for the first few days. After that, silent questions shot back and forth in our eyes. What had happened? Where had they gone? How had they done it?

We were professionals. If we couldn't find them, then they must not be in the immediate area and if they weren't in the immediate area, where were they?

As the days wore on with endless searching, the answer became, "We don't care, as long as they're out of *our* turf."

Lack of action in combat turns a young man's head toward action of the heart.

The pilots in our unit were young, few were married, and most were in love with someone at home whose face they could remember only by looking at a photograph.

Letters were written back and forth, but as time wore on they usually became fewer and fewer and shorter and shorter.

The letters we wrote described things we saw and experiences we had to people living in an entirely different universe: home. We couldn't expect them to understand what we did or why.

Reading their letters and remembering what it was like to be home doing family stuff—getting a burger, seeing a real movie with someone special—would make you momentarily crazy. And that momentary craziness could get you or someone else killed. So, you read it, put it away, and forgot. Just as you wrote it, mailed it, and tried not to remember. Little wonder the boys were out looking for something more tangible.

Girls.

Eight days after Ripcord, about dusk, I was fulfilling a personal duty, writing to my mother who was living on our farm in Yakima, Washington. I wrote about the safe issues, the wonderful weather we were having and how nice this place might be if everyone wasn't trying so hard to do bodily harm to everyone else.

Just then an orderly came in. "Excuse me, lieutenant, but I've got a problem. Can you help me?"

I wasn't known as a procedure sort of fellow, so to have a desk clerk ask me for help was interesting enough in itself to put aside a letter home for a minute.

"Sure, corporal, what can I do for you?"

"Well, sir," he said, "it's like this. The commanding officer (CO) is at the general mess and says he doesn't exist tonight. The executive officer (XO) is passed out at the club."

He paused. "Well, it seems some of the 'slick' pilots took a transport helicopter and went to the 85th," the clerk continued. "Rumor has it that there is a party at the 85th SMASH hospital including real US Army nurses."

"It seems to me, corporal, the CO gave us all pretty much a laundry day for tomorrow," I said. "Where's the problem?"

"Well, sir," he went on, "the CO of the 85th called. Not only is the ship they flew over parked on the ramp in front of the emergency room so no one else can get in, but the guys are, shall we say, too impaired to move it. He's rather serious about having the aircraft repositioned back over here but prefers he didn't wind up having a mass casualty situation on the ramp, if you know what I mean."

"Great," I said. "By the way, how many of our pilots are over there?"

"Fifteen, sir."

"Oh, Lord! And what does he expect us to do?"

"He'd like us to send over a couple someones who are sober enough to fly them home and who have enough rank to kick fanny. All I could find was you."

"Thanks," I said.

"He's on the phone, sir. It doesn't do any good to hang up. He just calls back. Could you, ah . . ."

"Sure," I said. "I'll be right there."

Sorry, Ma. Duty calls.

Just walking into the operations room I could feel the hostility. I picked up the phone, announced my name and rank and was greeted with, "A lieutenant!?"

I explained that nearly everyone else was a little misplaced that evening.

He told me he knew exactly where everyone was. They were in *his* club harassing *his* nurses.

Many apologies later, I said we'd be right over. I found two other reasonably straight pilots, jumped into a scout ship and we were off to the 85th SMASH.

As we landed, it seemed that the place was more brightly illuminated than usual. Then we saw why. Jeeps and headlights were everywhere. The MPs (military police) had a few of the boys in the back of the ship they had flown over. The other guys were being led across the ramp by several more police amid great shouting. Obviously, a good time was being had by all.

The 85th commanding officer, a full colonel, came over to me. "You the lieutenant I talked to on the ringer?"

"Yes, sir," I replied.

He had calmed down but informed me he wanted the other ship and guys out, and *now*, soldier. And I would go with him to inspect the damage to the club.

I sent the men home. The MPs left muttering under their breath something about pilots and their heritage.

When we got to the club, the party was still going on. The colonel showed me around while I made note of what was to be put in order tomorrow. The next thing I knew, we were chatting like old pals.

A Thai band was playing . . . reasonably well. Loud, but not badly. The colonel had walked off to attend to something. I sat down and then I saw her. The same nurse I'd spoken to when I was looking for Brian in the emergency room. I couldn't believe it. This was like something I'd read about in old novels—I was in love. Weak, flushed, heart pounding, in love!

She was dancing with a captain, a pilot yet! I couldn't take my eyes off her. She glanced my way. I looked down at the floor. My feelings were strange. I knew that I'd met her only once but it was like I had known her always. I was even jealous she was with someone else. And I didn't even know her name. I was still looking at the floor when I heard someone in the band say, "last dance."

I was trying, really trying, to figure a way to introduce myself when I felt someone tapping me on the shoulder. "Hi, would you like the last dance?" I looked up. She was standing beside me. I don't think I said anything. I just stood up and took her hand. On the dance floor I just wanted to hold her and stay like that forever. I knew my life had been touched by someone special. I would never again be the same. Gathering all my nerve, I asked her name. She was Patti Gingell from Euclid, Ohio, 1st Lieutenant, US Army, and she had been in the country for one month. When the music stopped we sat down together. Now what should I do? I couldn't just let everything end here. If we were back in the "world," we could always go somewhere in my old junker. This, of course, was not home.

Then I had one of my rare moments of pure genius. "Say, Patti, my helicopter is parked outside," I began. "It's a nice night. Would you be interested in seeing the lights of Hue city from the air?"

She thought for a moment and said, "Sure, I'd love to."

We walked over to my ship on the ramp. With great pleasure I buckled her into the co-pilot's seat. Since I usually kept my automatic rifle there, I asked her to hold it for me, explaining as I handed it to her that it was loaded.

I got in, fired up the turbine engine and we took off into a beautiful clear sky. Soon we were over Hue, a mysterious old city with a long and marvelous history, a city that was the embodiment of the Vietnam of yesterday. At least what was left of it.

Patti was wearing an extra flight helmet that I kept in the ship so we could talk without having to yell over the engine noise. As the walrus said, we talked of many things. Home, what had brought her to this war of lost souls, did she have a boyfriend? She said "no" to the question about the boyfriend but then asked about those "pretty little green things" that were going by the ship.

*Tracers!* Our first date had drawn enemy fire.

I reached up, switched off the outside running lights and the rotating beacon. Blacked out, I made a very tight turn.

Patti was totally unruffled. She locked a round into the chamber of my rifle, then turned to me and asked, "Shall I return fire, John?"

"No, dear, that isn't necessary," I said. "They can't see us now."

What a girl! In the two situations we had shared, she had handled both calmly, coolly, and rationally. She was not only beautiful and intelligent but brave to boot.

We flew back to the 85th SMASH. Later, as we walked slowly to the nurses quarters, I asked if I could see her again. She said she would enjoy that and gave me an idea of her schedule so that I would know when she would not be working. I hardly needed a helicopter to fly home that night.

The next day I went to my commanding officer. He was the sort of fellow that any trooper would follow anywhere, any time. He wasn't rank conscious. Besides being an authority figure, he seconded as being the older brother or father who wasn't otherwise available.

I told him about Patti, how I thought I felt and that I would like to see her whenever possible. I asked if that was acceptable, could I use a ship to fly back and forth? It was not unlike asking Dad for the keys to the car.

He laughed, and looking at me knowingly, told me that we would try it on a temporary basis but I had better not be late for missions!

I could have hugged him but managed to restrain myself.

Patti and I had a truly whirlwind romance. Seeing Patti became anything but temporary.

For the next few months we saw each other as much as possible. I would fly over when she was off duty and we would just walk, talk, sit in the sun, or huddle together under a poncho when it rained.

Patti was deeply religious and loved children. When the roads out of her camp were open and secure, she went to a nearby orphanage operated by Catholic nuns. She brought gifts of soap, clothes, and whatever toys she could take to the children. I went along just to watch their little faces light up when she arrived. I understood. She made me feel good, too.

Patti's visits to my unit brought more good feelings. Immediately, clean uniforms were everywhere and staring replaced swearing as a favorite pastime. Everyone loved to talk to her, some just to hear the sound of a real American girl's voice. She was glad to talk and to listen.

Every day that Patti visited our unit was special. But of all these days, one stood out above the others. Patti had decided to hitchhike to my main base. Standing on the road in front of her hospital she flagged a truck. She told the driver where she wanted to go and without any more questions they were off.

When they arrived at my unit, I was sitting on the steps of my hootch. I saw a string of trucks with Patti, waving, in the lead vehicle. The truck that had picked her up had been followed by the convoy behind it. The parade of vehicles made an impressive sight.

When it stopped in front of my barracks, Patti opened the door of the first transport. Waving to each in turn, she said her "thank yous" to the entire group that had unknowingly taken a long detour. Like me, they would have followed her anywhere.

We had just kissed "hello" when I saw another parade approaching. Enlisted men from my platoon, Bill in the lead, were all walking up to the steps where Patti had just sat down next to me.

Bill requested permission to speak to Patti.

"Shall I leave?" I asked.

"No, sir. This is for you, too."

"Then granted," I said.

Clearing his throat, Bill read a poem the men had written to Patti. That done, they presented her with a handdrawn certificate designating her an honorary scout pilot. It was beautifully done and they had obviously taken a great deal of pride in their work.

They had decided that as a scout pilot, she needed a call sign. Banshee, my call sign, was not fitting for such a lady. After taking a vote, they had chosen "Angel." And being superstitious people, they had added the number seven.

"Angel 7." She was their luck.

From that time on, when someone asked about Patti, it was Angel 7. They loved her because I loved her. They also loved her just because she was lovable.

When I flew Patti back to her unit that night, I found time to play a little mind game on the air traffic controller at Phu Bai.

All conversations between arriving or departing aircraft and the Phu Bai control tower were basic and set. When I said one thing, I expected a certain response. This was procedure. Nothing more.

We were approaching Phu Bai. Unknown to Patti, I had already written down on a piece of paper who was to say what to whom on the radio. I switched the aircraft radio-talk switch to the co-pilot side, handed her the note and over the intercom asked her to read it.

"Saber Tower," she said, "this is Angel 7. We are inbound from Camp Eagle at 1500 feet. We are one mile out for landing at the 85th. Guns are locked off."

I wish that I could have been inside that tower to see the man's face. The radio was silent for awhile. Then we heard, "Angel 7, Saber Tower. Permission granted for landing at the 85th and thank you."

His thanks were genuine. To him, whether her voice had been real or imagined, it was a welcome change from the usual male staccato.

# Chapter 2

On those other days when Patti arrived at my unit while I was flying, she would sometimes sit on the steps of the scout hootch and wait for our return. She always brought a book with her to read while waiting. She normally ended up spending her time talking and listening to the other scouts and our gunners.

The flight line personnel always seemed to know what was happening, even if we didn't. Certainly they knew whether or not Patti was on the property. They also knew that she would want to know when we were returning home.

At the sound of our team's return, someone on the flight line would ring our hootch and tell whoever answered, "Please tell Angel 7 that they're approaching."

When Patti was known to be on site, a few of the men in the unit, knowing where she was usually waiting, would hang out by the radio room. When they heard my lead Cobra radio when we were inbound, "two minutes out for touch down," several of those men would go sit, stand, or walk slowly to the steep dirt trail that ran along the little hill between our hootch and where we parked our aircraft.

As Patti walked along that narrow trail toward our flight line, there was always at least one trooper waiting to give her a helping hand in the more difficult spots. She never really needed their assistance but accepted with her usual smile. What better good could a trooper do than give an angel a reassuring hand? There was little more that could improve a trooper's day.

Unless, of course, it was one of those days when Patti brought several of her friends with her to visit.

Patti mentioned to the other nurses at her unit one day that, given the opportunity, they should consider coming with her to visit our Cavalry unit. It would be, at the least, a change of environment. She explained that, despite all the horror stories they had heard about Air Cavalry troopers, she was always treated as a friend, a lady, and the officer she was.

The nurses knew that Patti and I were deeply in love. They felt good being with us and being, in a way, a part of that love. It was our love that helped them overlook the fact that I was a Cav pilot, let alone a scout.

They also knew my gunner, Bill, from when he had been with me on occasional visits to the 85th Evac.

Later that evening they agreed that maybe they really did feel comfortable around the Cavalry. At least Bill and me. Amazing enough, several of the nurses thought of Bill as easy going and fun. I arrived a little later to visit and, over handmade pizza at Patti's, had two single nurses mention to me something about "that cute gunner Bill you fly with." I made the mistake of not knowing the whole conversation and then, startled, saying, "Cute? Bill who?" My answer came only a second before Patti's combat boot met my knee. I learned to sit and, under the threat of pain, just nod my head in the affirmative when Bill's name was mentioned. (However, I must now go on record that I did not then, nor do I now, think of Bill as "cute." I can only hope he feels the same about me.)

If the nurses visited and were really worried, they could just stay around Patti, Bill, and me they decided. It would be a learning experience. It might even turn out to be fun. The nurses agreed that they might visit.

Someday.

Someday came two days later.

Our commanding officer, concerned about battle damage to our ships and a bit of a morale problem due to daily combat, ordered our unit to "stand down" for forty-eight hours. This meant that we were not available for combat duties during that period. We were to devote our attention to caring for our aircraft and, somehow, raising our spirits.

The CO, aware of the fact that a pilot with a tool in his hand could do more damage to an aircraft than any enemy division, ordered us aviators just to stay out of the way. "Be on the flight line but don't interfere. Let maintenance do their jobs, just give support," he said.

Shortly after his order was issued, I came to the CO's office to drop off a report. When worried, he had an occasional habit of talking out loud to himself. Not knowing, or caring that anyone else was there, he said out loud, "What should I do about morale?"

Thinking only of myself and, of course, wanting Patti to visit, I knocked on his door. I excused myself for bothering him then immediately mentioned the conversation Patti had had with the other nurses during my earlier visit to the 85th Evac. I did not bring up Bill's name.

I explained that some of the nurses might enjoy visiting our unit. If he would allow it, what more could he do for morale? Being in his late 30s, I wasn't sure he knew what I was driving at.

"Well, it sounds like a pretty good idea. I'll call their CO. I sure hope he's forgotten some of the recent past," he said.

Call he did.

The 85th Evacuation Hospital commanding officer hadn't forgotten anything.

Regardless, peace terms were negotiated; arrangements were made.

Rules were set in stone.

Because of the lack of casualties, "maybe due to the fact your people aren't flying," the 85th CO stated, our chief was told that Patti and four other "volunteer" nurses would be allowed onto our compound.

One of their medical helicopters would drop them off in the morning and pick them up before dark. I guess someone had already said something about Patti and me going on a night flight and the "green things."

Our CO would guarantee their safety.

The necessary promises were made. The deal was done.

The next morning, everyone in our unit was doing just as ordered—be on the flight line. There was a real lack of energy though. "Hanging around" would be a good term. No one was putting much effort into anything, just going through the motions of looking busy.

Suddenly, the sirens that usually meant one of our aircraft was "down" began blaring. Everybody ran to their respective ships before we realized none of us were on missions.

The sirens stopped.

It was our CO's strange way of getting our attention.
As we stood by our ships, a medivac ship landed on our flight line.

Off stepped Patti and four other nurses.

The medivac helicopter departed quickly.

Thirty men of the elite Air Cavalry stood frozen.

Having an idea about what had happened, I walked over to Patti and escorted her to my ship.

Bill followed my lead. "This way ladies. Let me give you a tour."

As Bill showed them around, Patti and I stood side by side. Steve and Mike, two other veteran scout pilots, walked over and asked Patti if she knew what was going on.

"Sure," Patti said, "It's a mingling of cultures. Most nurses believe you guys are animals. Prove otherwise."

Bill introduced the nurses to the entire unit. Unfortunately both the troops and the nurses felt awkward. The ladies all soon found their way back to where Patti and I were sitting next to my aircraft.

Steve collected lawn chairs for everyone and several coolers filled with sodas. Except for a few "thank yous," there was little more conversation.

It was a hot day; the sun blazed.

Patti, knowing things were not going well, walked over to a couple helicopters, grabbed some flak-jackets and set them on top of the nearby protective revetments. She took two more from my ship, put them next to my aircraft, took off her jacket, rolled up her jungle fatigue pants, and began enjoying the sun. To her friends she said, "If you're going to sun bathe in a war zone, can you imagine a safer place?"

Seeing her having fun, the other nurses decided that maybe the situation wasn't so bad. Two others began taking in the sun from lawn chairs.

The other nurses began walking around, looking at the aircraft and asking questions. The gunners and mechanics enjoyed explaining how everything worked. Everyone relaxed. Men and women. Officers and enlisted. The day went on. Food from our mess hall was brought down to the flight line. We all ate together, talked, and laughed.

It was fun. It became a picnic.

Morale soared. Ours and, hopefully, theirs.

Then Rick rolled in.

Rick was a pilot who had come to the unit several months before my arrival. He had volunteered for scouts. After three days, he quit. As he was fond of saying, "It wasn't my ball of wax." Being a pilot who not only lacked ability but also initiative, he was assigned to a low position in our maintenance section. No matter. He was usually a nice person. At least I liked him. Like all of us, he just wanted to go home alive.

Rick managed to create a lot of free time for himself. That free time was spent in the mess hall. He was naturally heavyset. As time went on he became, to use the term loosely, large.

Very large.

His nickname became Huge Rick. It was never said to his face but it was his nickname nonetheless.

Anyway, there we all were, enjoying the sun, food, company, and idle chatter when Rick showed up. Being ever polite, Rick explained that he needed to do a test flight on an aircraft that happened to be parked right in the middle of where we all now stood. He would try not to 'dust' us on takeoff. We asked him to wait an hour or so. "No. Please move." We did.

Something should be explained at this point. In the art of helicopter flying, there are many things that need to be touched, kicked, looked at, questioned, and generally considered before starting the turbine engine and lifting off for flight.

One of these things is a little factor known as center of gravity. If the weight of the aircraft fuel in the rear is low and there is an exceptionally heavy weight in the cockpit up front, there is a real good chance that, when the ship breaks ground for takeoff, the nose of the ship will drop. The center of gravity being too far forward, the aircraft will uncontrollably move forward. There will not be enough aft stick (cyclic) to bring the nose up.

Rick, being the sort of pilot he was, touched, kicked, and looked at nothing. He just got in and fired her up. His fuel was low—very low. Rick provided the catalyst to ignite the problem. His weight.

His first saving grace was that he wasn't parked in an aircraft revetment. He had requested earlier that the ship be pulled out onto the narrow runway between our two sets of protective barriers on either side of the landing strip.

Unfortunately, that narrow runway was where about thirty aircrew and five nurses stood.

Rick picked up to a hover. He immediately began moving forward. He picked up speed and, in a flash, was on the ride of his life.

One of the nurses asked if we all flew that crazy.

"Only on purpose," I answered, "and I don't think this is on purpose."

Steve had just joined several of us with an extra lawn chair he had found. A maintenance sergeant walked over and said, "Excuse me, sirs, but I don't think that takeoff was a good idea. I was told to drain all but ten gallons of fuel from that ship."

Knowingly, Steve looked at me and rolled his eyes.

I've got to give Rick credit. Like him or not, he didn't panic. However, his command decision to attempt a landing right back onto the little hover landing strip he had just departed—and where we all stood—rather than maneuvering to our main field nearby was, in my mind, irresponsible.

Whatever his reasoning, here he came. Just as irresponsibly, none of us moved. We couldn't believe he would try to land in front of us.

He tried.

Rick and his aircraft screamed past us. Fifty feet away, and a good 80 mph, the toes of his skids touched down on the metal runway. There was a major shower of sparks. This continued for another hundred yards or so until Rick had the presence of mind to chop his flight throttle and retard his engine RPM. His roller coaster ride stopped sliding and, power reduced, sat level on the ground. He shut everything down.

A very shaken Rick struggled out of the small cockpit. He walked all the way to our wide-eyed group, grabbed the first nurse he saw and kissed her on the lips.

That nurse was, by chance, one who hadn't really felt good about the visit several nights before.

Being the nice guy he was, Rick proceeded, embarrassed, to introduce himself to the now even more surprised lady. "Oh, sorry. My name is Rick. Sorry. Thank you. Thanks, thanks . . . " As he walked away, all we heard was, "thanks, thanks . . . thanks," until we couldn't hear him anymore.

The nurse Rick had kissed turned to Patti and said, "Well, you promised us a good time and a change of pace. So far, so good."

All too soon, evening arrived. A medivac helicopter returned to pick up our visitors.

Although we were all sad to see them leave, everyone seemed to return to work with a renewed sense of dedication. Later, after the medivac returned the nurses to their unit, Patti telephoned our CO to thank him for inviting them over. Several of the nurses also thanked our CO, then asked to say hello to individual troopers they had met. Our phone lines were tied up for hours.

If you shut your eyes real tight and pretended, you could almost believe we were home.

It was a good day.

During those few months, we never talked about our jobs. The consequences of my being shot down, killed or, worst yet in my mind, captured, were never mentioned. Talk of the occasional rocket attack upon the hospital and something happening to Patti never entered our conversations or the world we created when we were together. For those moments, ours was a happy life full of hope and peace.

Nor did we speak of the growing love between us. We both knew what was happening but it didn't seem right to put that love into words.

Despite our fantasy world, there was a real war full of death and horror going on around us. We both knew in our hearts that to say "I love you" and then to have one of us lose the other would have made that loss an unbearable tragedy. We had already seen and been part of enough tragedy.

# Chapter 3

I was lying on my cot in my little five-foot-by-eight-foot room in the scout hootch. I was reading a book about Buddhism that my mother had sent me. Mother was always expanding her horizons and had sent me the book "for consideration."

I was somewhere between sleep and trying to focus on the book's small print when the ringer on the phone in our hootch made noise. Being the only pilot around, I slowly got up and answered the hated mission phone. "Hello!" I yelled into my end. "Get yourself up here now sir. The boss—excuse me—the CO wants you," our company clerk said.

Sometimes I wanted to wring the clerk's neck. I think he called every now and then just to make us walk up the hill that stood between us and the rest of our unit.

During my trek up the hill, I was having trouble understanding what was going on. Mike had just left for a mission so it wasn't my turn yet. No sirens had gone off, so no downed ship. What was the deal?

I found out soon enough.

When I arrived at the commander's office, I saw him walking around in small, tight circles. He was nervous. That made me nervous.

"Look, John, here's what we have," the CO said. "An infantry trooper was picked up by medivac helicopter this morning. He was slightly wounded. On the way to the 85th, the ship picked up five others who had just been wounded, only more seriously. When the ship arrived at the 85th, the slightly wounded soldier pulled a weapon on the pilots. He says he wants to go home. He won't let anyone near the ship until he gets fuel enough to fly the ship to Da-Nang and a promise of a trip back to the world. The other wounded need help and need help now. They can't wait for Da-Nang. There's no assurance they'll even get that far if he's that nuts."

He looked at me hard. "There's a negotiator talking to him now," he continued.

"Yes, sir, I understand. What can I do?" I asked.

"John," he said, "no pilot knows the 85th quite as well as you. You should. You spend more time there than here. Anyway, I want you to fly a Special Forces sniper into position—as close to the helipad as you can get him. You know what I mean. Close enough to get a clear shot. The job stinks."

"Yes, sir. I'll get my gear," I answered.

"Forget your gear. The sniper is in your ship and waiting. Just go!"

"I'm on the way," I said.

"No," he called. "Wait. There's more." He paused. "Patti's the negotiator. She was the first person to arrive at the medivac when it landed. She managed to help one of the wounded off the ship before he put a gun to the pilot's head. Patti's been talking to the bad guy for some time now. I hear he trusts her."

"You should also know," he continued, "that he points his pistol at Patti when he gets aggravated. Get over there. Pick a good position."

Without answering, I turned and ran out the door. I slowed to a fast walk a few strides later. I knew that if I began to get too excited, I was in jeopardy of doing something stupid. This had to be just another mission.

Yards from my aircraft I could hear Bill yelling at the top of his lungs, "Get out of my aircraft, you maggot! I'll kill you where you sit!"

I knew Bill could be mean. I also knew that it was most likely the Special Forces sniper that Bill was screaming at. Those guys took the word mean and multiplied it by ten.

"Bill," I ordered as I got closer, "it's OK! You stay here. This job goes without you. I'll explain later."

"OK, LT, but I don't like this guy sitting in my seat without asking," Bill said. Looking the sniper in his eyes, he said, "I'll be here when my lieutenant brings you back."

As I climbed into my cockpit, I looked into my back seat where Bill usually sat. I saw an individual in total camouflage. The eyes that my gunner had looked into were all that was exposed. Over his jungle uniform, he wore a covering of loose, flapping shreds of various shades of brown and green cloth. I had heard stories of these guys sitting days without moving, waiting for enemy troops to move along suspected trails. The enemy would hear shots fired, see friends fall, but never locate the man behind the weapon. They were one with the jungle.

I started my turbine, waving Bill away as I increased power.

We were only minutes away from the 85th as soon as we lifted off from my base. I tried to focus on my passenger. He wasn't wearing a flight helmet, so I couldn't talk to him on the radio. I leaned out my door and, looking back, started to ask loudly how close he needed to be. I found myself looking into the barrel of a very powerful hunting rifle and an even more powerful scope.

I figured distance was not to be a concern.

We approached the 85th from the north. I gave Saber Tower nothing more than my call-sign. They had been contacted by land line and were aware of my mission.

All other air traffic was being diverted until the "situation was solved."

We landed in a local farmer's small garden about 150 yards from the hospital heliport. I was in short and to-the-point radio contact with the hospital radio room. They didn't indicate any change in the situation. I couldn't ask about Patti. I didn't know if the person causing the problem had access to an aircraft flight helmet and radio.

Our landing prompted my passenger to physically move for the first time. He stepped slowly from my ship. Where I fought my way through the mud, he seemed to glide as if on ice.

There was a small dike immediately between us and the target. It was there that he set up a firing position. I lay down next to him and considered wiping off forty pounds of added weight in mud that was stuck to my boots. I didn't, but I couldn't help notice my sniper friend was perfectly clean.

"You any good?" I asked.

No response.

There we sat for maybe twenty minutes in real time, an eternity in my mind.

Then the sniper just stood up, dusted off his weapon, and moving as easily as before, returned to the aircraft.

After struggling through the mud to reach my ship, I screamed at him, "What happened? You never fired a shot. What happened?"

"Home," he said. "Mission over."

"This mission is over when I say it's over!" I yelled as I started the engine and took off.

I radioed the hospital, "This is John! What happened? Is Patti all right?"

"John! We've been trying to raise you!" I was told. "Patti's fine. Come on over. Just be careful. There are a lot of MPs running around."

Come over we did.

We landed in the middle of everyone, MPs and all. I didn't care. I think I even surprised my passenger.

Although we more or less barged our way in, we were not allowed to talk to Patti. Investigators were debriefing her. She saw me and waved weakly.

There were other people milling around that I knew. They told me the story.

Two helicopters with wounded were on the hospital pads. There was room for only two transports at a time.

When the aircraft carrying the slightly wounded soldier and other more seriously wounded arrived, their ship was forced to wait until another ship departed and made landing space. That's when he became upset. His helicopter landed in the next available spot. He pulled a weapon and threatened the pilots. He wanted to be flown home.

Patti was already walking out to the ship to let the wounded soldiers know they would be soon cared for. That's when the weapon was pointed at her.

He made threats. He wanted to go home he said again. Now!

He would kill the pilots. He would kill her.

As hospital personnel approached to off-load the wounded, Patti carefully motioned them away. All they did was slow down, not understanding.

Turning from the weapon being pointed at her, Patti informed the stretcher bearers behind her there was a problem. Now seeing the weapon, they returned to the emergency room.

The next person out was the chief nurse. She was about fifteen feet from Patti when the gunman said that he didn't want to see or deal with anyone but Patti—or else! The chief nurse backed away.

It was not much later that my sniper friend was just getting his windage. Before he could sight in his target, Patti took control of the situation.

Speaking softly and gently, she convinced him to lay down his weapon. Why should anyone else be hurt? There were already others dying. They needed help.

Please?

Trusting her, he walked to Patti and gave her his weapon. She threw it to her side onto the ground and, arms open, hugged him.

Together they turned and began walking toward the emergency room.

Now disarmed, dozens of military police pounced on him, knocking both him and Patti to the ground.

Patti yelled for them to leave him alone. Her pleas fell on deaf ears. She was cut and bruised in the scuffle. When Patti was able to stand, she was visibly upset.

That night, as Patti and I held each other tight, we thought we were the only two people that were sane in a world gone crazy.

The sniper? I never saw him again.

✦ ✦ ✦

Two events that followed in quick succession made me consider changing my mind about total commitment to this lady who had become so much a part of my life.

First, I was shot down again. Bill and I had been sent on a recon mission at first light into the A Shau Valley bordering Laos. We called it the "Valley of the Dead." It was an appropriate name.

Our work was marked by two particularly hazardous moments. One was leaving the formation and the protection of the Cobras and going to treetop level. It left us exposed to enemy fire. The other was completing the mission and going back to the other ships. Again, we were exposed.

The mission was about over and the cover ships had told me to come up to the altitude where they were circling. We were just left of a ridge line and beginning to climb when I saw a puff of smoke from the perimeter of a small jungle clearing below and to my left.

I knew instantly what it was. A rocket propelled grenade. Even before the explosion, I was yelling "taking fire!"

The rocket went off just below and behind me, spraying shrapnel everywhere. It lifted our helicopter up on its nose.

Bill was shooting at anything and everything. I was shouting on the radio. We both smelled smoke.

The really bad news came next. The engine quit. "Banshee 14, flame out, going in!"

The Cobras had gotten behind me, seen where I was going and, in their infinite wisdom, began firing rockets past me into the clearing ahead. I could only hope their fire power would convince the present tenants to leave.

My landing, quite honestly, was almost textbook perfect. As I turned off switches and grabbed a fire extinguisher, I saw something that provoked more hysterical laughter from me than anything has before or since.

Bill, whose duty it was to set up a defensive position once on the ground, had grabbed an armful of grenades, his machine gun, and ammo to protect us and the ship.

He had forgotten, however, to disconnect the radio wire that ran from his flight helmet to a very long extension wire connected to the inside of the ship.

As he was running, the wire came taut. Grenades, gun, and ammo, plus Bill with feet in the air, went flying.

It took a second for the scene to register in my mind, but when it did, I couldn't stop laughing. Tears came to my eyes.

There we were, on the ground, in enemy territory, rockets from the Cobras going off all around, ship burning, and me laughing like a crazy man.

Adrenaline and fear are a strong mixture.

Tears or not, I got the fire out and took a look at the damage. It didn't seem bad.

I got back into the cockpit, and after a few hurried promises to the powers that be (that I knew I'd never keep), hit the engine ignite button. It started!

Meanwhile, Bill had gathered his gear and was standing on the skid while I told the Cobras we were coming out. They covered us and we climbed out under their rocket and cannon protection.

It was on the way back that I thought if I had been killed, I would have died never having told Patti how much I loved her.

The second event only strengthened what I had realized after the first. Bill and I, again in the A Shau Valley, were flying down a dirt road that ran much of the valley's length. It seemed no matter how often the Air Force blew it up, the enemy rebuilt it.

The hour was early when Bill noticed an area of road that looked recently worked. He saw that the dirt was a little fresher and damper where it cut through a small rise, not unlike unfinished bunkers.

Bill suggested flying down the road just off to one side while he fired 40 mm grenades into the holes. It seemed like a good idea at the time.

Bill had fired about three grenades into holes with no results. Then, as he was about to fire again, three enemy soldiers popped up in front of me. I pulled the trigger on my mini-gun just as Bill fired at another hole. Then the whole world seemed to explode.

His grenade had hit a hidden ammo cache. The ship was hit hard with a shower of shrapnel on the right side. I was surprised to hear myself on the radio saying, "I'm wounded."

The right side of my face was numb. The Cobras covered our escape and climb out.

I looked down and saw blood dripping onto my shirt. I turned to Bill. "How bad am I hit?"

He was as white as a sheet. "Oh, jeez, John. Oh jeez. , You're bleeding!"

I already knew that. The ship was running fine, but I told the Cobras I felt a little lightheaded.

I'm sure this was not very comforting to Bill in the back seat.

The Cobras fell into a protective formation and escorted me to the nearest friendly firebase. A rescue ship picked me up and flew me to a hospital. The 85th SMASH.

A funny thing happened on the way to the hospital.

When Bill and I were transferred to the medical aircraft, I had not been given time to shut down my aircraft engine. I had left the helicopter running in the flight idle mode.

While en route to the hospital, a Cobra pilot radioed our rescue ship and requested engine shutdown procedures for my aircraft. He had landed nearby my parked ship.

Sheepishly, I gave them to him.

Of course, Bill had to add his two cents worth.

"Hey, LT," Bill spouted, "don't be embarrassed about leaving a reasonably good helicopter still running in the middle of a small landing zone (LZ). Unless it's in the air providing cover to the infantry there, it's just junk. Tell the Snake jockey not to bother shutting her down. The guys on that LZ will probably blow her in place."

Bill was wrong.

They did not "blow her in place."

They did later that afternoon, however, push it over the hill on their perimeter to provide landing room for a transport helicopter that was bringing in hot rations.

Unknown to me at the time, Patti had come over to our unit during my mission. She had planned lunch together after my return to base.

My CO had thought that she might like to listen to the mission I was flying on our operations radio. It would give her an idea of what I did for a living, he reasoned.

Reluctantly, she had agreed. She heard everything. When I announced over the radio that I had been wounded, she asked to be flown to the hospital to wait for me. She was, indeed, waiting.

I was carried from the rescue ship to a table in the emergency room. My flight helmet was taken off and there it was for all to see: a small piece of shrapnel in my cheek that had done nothing more than make me bleed like a stuck pig. I had cut myself worse just shaving.

It was removed with tweezers. I got two stitches and sat up to see Patti.

"Hi," I said.

"Don't 'hi' me. And don't ever scare me like that again! Now come on, let's get some lunch." The subject was dropped and never mentioned again. We walked on. Again I didn't tell her that I loved her.

What if it had been this time and I had been killed? She never would have heard that I wanted her not only for now, but forever. We walked on in silence.

A few days later, the CO told me that there were some rest and relaxation slots available. I had been in-country long enough to qualify.

"Home. Can I go home for a few days?"

"Sure," he said. "Ten days actually."

I didn't want to leave Patti, even for one day, but this seemed a way to answer questions that had been nagging me. Was I just using her as a shield against all the destruction going on around me? Was I being honest with her or myself? Was it love or convenience? I had to know.

To know, I had to escape this environment and evaluate my true feelings in a sane setting. "OK, sign me up, sir."

"Fine," he replied. "You go out in two days. Say hello to the world for me."

I flew over to the hospital that night and told Patti that I was going home for a few days. She was on duty, so we had only a few minutes. I explained that it was an opening that had just become available.

She listened quietly, green eyes unblinking. Inside I knew she believed that I was going home to someone else. Then she kissed me and said, "I'll see you when you get back. Now (softly) I have work to do."

The flight back to base was very lonely.

# Chapter 4

I don't know whether anyone who hasn't been there can understand the culture shock of going from war to peace. One day I was a flying target for enemy fire. Then I was transported to Da Nang Air Base on a bus with grenade-proof chicken wire windows. Next I boarded a real passenger jet, took a long nap, and woke up close to home. The experience was mind boggling.

My first tour of duty in Vietnam had ended abruptly with a bad wound. Then I went home in stages. I had time to think about it. First Saigon, then Japan, then California, and finally the nearest military hospital to home. In my case, Fort Lewis, Washington. In comparison, this was unbelievable.

When I got off the shuttle flight in Yakima, a strange sensation came over me. Everything was the same but also very different. Then I realized why. All my primary senses were operating at peak performance. They had to where I had been. They gave me the little extra advantage I needed to stay alive.

The sky in Yakima had never been bluer, the sounds never clearer, the smells so pure, or the food so good. The ground under my feet had never been so familiar or as reassuring. Better yet, I knew that as long as I stayed off First Street, chances were nobody would shoot at me.

Due to my unexpectedly fast travel time, I had not had a chance to contact home and let Mom know that I was on my way. I grabbed a taxi, which was not difficult at that time in Yakima. Of the four cabs in town, at least three were always, for some unknown reason, at the airport planes or no planes.

On the way to the farm I remembered an old Gary Cooper movie. As a soldier arriving home after World War I, he walked up a road leading to his family farmhouse. There he found his surprised but happy mother.

Being somewhat sentimental, I asked to be let out at the beginning of our long driveway. And there was Mom! It was a shock to us both and a moment neither of us will ever forget. Bless Gary Cooper!

It was a day of many hugs and kisses. A continual dialing of the phone, hearing Mom giggle, "Guess who's home!" and two hours of "Here, eat this, you're just bones. Don't they feed you?"

Later, when everything calmed down and family and friends had either gone home or were chatting in the kitchen, I took a walk in our peach orchard. It had always been my favorite place to walk and think.

As I watched the sun go down, I knew this was where Patti and I belonged. Together. Forever. I would ask her to be my wife. When I went to bed soon after, the sun I had just watched setting was now rising over Patti.

I love my family intensely and I know that they love me, but those ten days were trying for all concerned. They wanted to do things with me and for me.

All I wanted was to get back to Patti. I didn't try to explain to them about Patti and me because I needed to know whether Patti would accept my proposal. Maybe she didn't feel the same way I did.

The days did pass and, with regret, I said goodbye to my family. At the same time, it was with joy that I knew where I was going and to whom. For the first time, I understood that there was indeed a purpose for my being in this war. It was to meet Patti.

The same speedy efficiency that had brought me home returned me to Saigon.

When I arrived, I was told that all flights north, where I needed to go, had been canceled. The reason: "Big operation going on up there." Nobody could get out. Only equipment and supplies could get in. The more I asked, "What's really going on?" the more different answers I heard.

I had found out early on, during my first tour, that if I wanted information or needed help, the place to go was an Air Force Officers Club. When I noticed the main club on the air base in Saigon, I knew just what I was looking for inside.

Two separate groups of pilots were at the bar. One was a group of young guys. Noisy, flight suits, sunglasses, hands waving in the air recreating heroic maneuvers of daring and skill, and drinking shots of flaming tequila. The other was an older group of quieter men, slightly heavier in stature, bellies up to the bar, wearing flowered Hawaiian shirts and drinking Scotch.

Members of the first group were fighter pilots and rarely had time for a lowly helicopter pilot. Rumor had it that even when they were shot down they would ask our college alma mater before getting in one of our ships to be rescued. In the other group were transport pilots and they made time for anyone who would talk about something other than aviation.

I sat down next to a fellow with a particularly loud shirt. "Hi," I said.

"Hi, Army," he answered. The ice was broken.

"Can I buy you a drink?" I asked.

"Sure."

After a while I explained that I had just come in from leave and "What's going on up north?"

He told me there had been a massive build-up for an invasion into Laos. All the necessary troops were up there in position. Only support equipment was being flown in that direction.

"Are you by chance going to Phu Bai any time soon?" I asked. Phu Bai was where Patti's unit was based.

"Yeah, tomorrow morning," he said.

Time for my big pitch. "Look," I said, "I'm a scout pilot and I have quite a collection of captured enemy weapons and stuff I use for trading. I've got AKs, a couple of SKSs, a 30 cal., pith helmets, a flag, uniforms, and two officer's pistols. One with CCCP on the handle. (The CCCP engraving identified it as a Russian-made officer's weapon.) If you can get me to Phu Bai with you tomorrow, the pistols and whatever else you want are yours."

I thought I would have to wipe the drool off of his chin. He knew how much that stuff was worth in the right market. I would get what I wanted. A ticket to Patti.

We struck the deal with a handshake. We never let each other out of eye shot the entire night.

The next morning, after what seemed like only two hours' sleep (maybe it was only two hours sleep), we were in a C-130 transport full of rations and ammo on our way north. As we neared Phu Bai the pilot switched to my company radio frequency and I made contact with my unit.

Steve, a lieutenant/pilot and a very good friend, happened to respond. I explained that I was in a C-130, could they fly over to Phu Bai and pick me up that night and, by the way, bring my entire collection of "stuff."

"Your *whole* collection?" he asked.

"Yes, I'll explain later."

The Air Force pilot was grinning from ear to ear. A deal is a deal.

We arrived in Phu Bai and I made arrangements to meet the transport pilot that evening for the exchange of goods. Then I was on my way to the 85th SMASH.

People were scurrying all around. They seemed to be getting ready for lots of patients.

I asked around and was told that Patti was assisting in surgery. I went there and waited outside. Almost an hour later she walked out to see me. "John, you're back!" she said. "I thought I would never see you again."

"Patti, you may want to think about this, but I love you. Will you marry me?"

I remember hugs, I remember excitement, but to this day, I don't remember hearing what she said. Yes or no? Having asked her to marry me, and my being very tired, had totally drained me.

She went back to work and I went to the Officers' Mess to sit. Two hours later a nurse came in and congratulated me. As others came off duty, they did the same.

It was true! She must have said yes. And she had.

We had a small party that night in the nurses' quarters. I'd had enough presence of mind to bring back ten boxes of make-it-yourself pizzas. We cooked them in a pan over a butane heater.

Patti was radiant. Never before had she been more beautiful. Shortly, though, there was a knock at the door and Steve was saying, "Come on, man, we gotta go. The CO's got briefings scheduled for later."

Steve stopped long enough for a slice of pizza. I kissed Patti and promised I would be back tomorrow. Steve and I found the transport pilot and went to our helicopter.

The Air Force guy took the enemy weapons and items he wanted. Metal clanging on metal, he carried the stuff back to his own ship. He was giggling as he shuffled along under the weight.

I'm sure that even today there are some Air Force pilots gazing at those war souvenirs hanging over their fireplace mantels and telling dandy tales about them to their bored sons and daughters.

At our unit flight briefing that night we were told we were being held in reserve. Most of the main fighting was still a little farther northwest into Laos.

Although technically an invasion of Laos, the maneuver was more a show of force. There hadn't been as many casualties as expected and those were going to the hospital in Quan Tri, just south of the DMZ and to our north.

We scout pilots would not be involved in any night operations. That was good news. I could spend my evenings with Patti.

I did spend them with Patti. But it seemed we were also spending our time with the entire US Army. We had to go through the formality of asking our respective commanding officers for permission to marry. They gave it happily. Then we had to find a chaplain and chapel. Next came the paperwork. Tons and tons of paperwork. Permission from "higher" authority (whoever that was), State Department permission, and Vietnamese government permission. Next were the talks with the other nurses about who would be in the wedding party, where to get a cake, what to wear, what about announcements, the rings, and on and on.

Nothing was going to be easy, but everyone was getting involved. It became an *event*, and there wasn't a soul who wasn't thrilled to be a part of it all.

The invasion was soon completed. As so often happened, our forces withdrew in total, thus giving the territory back to the enemy.

I was flying about one mission a day and spending what time I could with Patti. Everything was relatively quiet in the combat sense of the word.

Word came that the Vietnamese government had granted our petition for marriage. This was not a ceremony, so to speak, but signing of affidavits. Still, it was a marriage.

We all gathered together in our finest jungle fatigues and drove to the specified government building. We were somewhat late.

We had to wait for some Viet Cong to be cleared from the area and the road declared secure. But we made it!

We went inside, showed our passports, swore to an oath read in Vietnamese, and signed a paper. We were married.

Although the Vietnamese wedding was just one of many steps that had to be taken in sequence before the US Army would marry us, the nurses who worked with Patti accepted it as the real thing. When we arrived back at the 85th SMASH, we found they had done a truly wonderful thing.

Because of her higher rank, one nurse had her own room. She gave that to us. Another, who had in her possession what must have been the only Sears double-sized mattress in Southeast Asia, put it in our new room. Others bartered for a small refrigerator, an air conditioner, and a hot plate.

These were all true gifts of the heart. Everyone saw what was happening between Patti and me as a thread of happiness in an otherwise unhappy and insane place.

At least, almost everyone was happy.

The hour was late. Patti and some of the nurses were going to her new quarters.

"I'll send for you soon," Patti said. "I want to be beautiful for you on this special night."

She already was, but, not to argue, I went over to the Officers' Club where some of the pilots had gathered. There were the expected lecherous comments and many stories of individual prowess. After awhile, one of Patti's friends came over.

"John, Patti would like to see you now."

The pilots applauded.

I adjusted my fatigues and proceeded across the compound to my new wife.

Just as I entered the nurses' area, I heard, "Where do you think you're going, lieutenant?" It was the chief of nursing.

"I'm going to see my new wife, the new Lieutenant Hendrix."

"I'm sorry, lieutenant," she said, "but nobody asked me about these new living arrangements and if they had, I wouldn't have approved. The Vietnamese may say that you are married but this is still US government property. Until the US Army says you are married, on this side of the fence, you are single. I'm just on the way to inform Lieutenant Gingell that she may keep her new room but you, soldier, stay out! Good night, lieutenant."

I knew then what it must feel like to get shot in the gut. There was nothing that I could say. She was a lieutenant colonel.

I went back to the club and explained to our friends what had happened. Some of the nurses went to console Patti. Later she came over to the club.

"Don't worry," she said. "We have all the rest of our lives."

What had I done to deserve so special a woman? Soon everyone went back to their quarters and the other pilots and I flew back to our main base.

✦ ✦ ✦

Shortly after our Vietnamese wedding, a new group of pilots arrived to replace earlier losses in my unit. As usual, most of these guys were Huey troop transport pilots, 'slick drivers' we called them. There were three exceptions. Two were Cobra pilots and one was, miraculously, a volunteer scout pilot.

These gentlemen were considered by other more experienced pilots either glory hunters or crazy or both. I hoped they were a little crazy. To me they were pure gold dipped in platinum and being crazy helped. If they wanted glory, they would have their fill of that soon enough.

The new pilots were a blessing from heaven. They could take some of the pressure off those of us who were left.

Casualties and transfers had taken their toll. The same number of missions had to be flown. Without replacements the slack had to be taken up by whoever was available.

The danger index skyrocketed with constant exposure to enemy fire. A new scout spelled relief and a new Snake pilot meant a fresh pair of eyes watching you work instead of two tired, burned holes.

Such was the pleasure of being with a volunteer unit.

When they arrived, I walked up the hill from our hootch to the orderly room to meet the new recruits. I had been told that Steve and Weird Bob, our experienced scouts, had already gone up to meet them.

As I approached the meeting place I saw Steve sitting on an ammo can wildly waving a cigarette and carrying on an animated conversation with nobody that I could see. His foot rested on an obviously occupied body bag.

I should have seen it coming. Steve didn't smoke.

I was about to ask what was going on when the new scout arrived escorted by an enlisted man who took one look at us and quickly disappeared.

Our latest arrival was just out of flight school. His uniform still had that special mothball aroma that only a new army uniform could have.

His name, rank, and unit patches weren't even sewn on yet. He was a kid. So were we. The only difference was that we had reached the war first.

I put out my hand to introduce myself and welcome him aboard. At this point Steve started yelling loudly into the empty air. "My poor trainee, he only made two missions!" he shouted, thumping the body bag with his foot.

Then Steve looked the new pilot straight in the eye. "So you want to be a scout pilot, do you?" he demanded.

Then he turned to me. "John, this time I get the new guy's insurance policy in *my* name. You got the last two. I have needs too, you know."

As I was about to ask, "What the . . . ?" Steve bent over and unzipped the body bag. There lay Weird Bob, playing dead, staring into space, his chest and face covered with red dye.

Steve was on a roll. "This is who you are replacing," he said, a finger wagging between Bob's blank stare and the recruit.

Our new pilot paled to a light shade of green, then flushed. In an instant, he turned on his heel and was gone. To the orderly room. To request a transfer. Scratch one scout.

Meanwhile, Steve and Weird Bob, still in his body bag, were rolling on the ground, howling with laughter. "Did you see him turn color?" Steve gasped.

"You know, that was great, man! What an act! We should be in vaudeville," Weird Bob managed between shrieks.

"Thanks, guys," I said. "That cost us. How do you clowns figure we're ever going to get any relief if you run off everyone before we even find out if they can fly? At least give them a chance to do the job. If they can't, fine; play your little games! This isn't a fraternity. It's a job. Personally, I'd like a coffee break now and then but without another pilot none of us will get one. Think about it!"

I might as well have talked to the wall. The two of them wandered off, arm-in-arm, marching in step and giggling like highschool kids.

Amazingly enough, not so long ago they had been in high school. What a war!

Like most officers, I had other chores to perform in addition to my normal missions. Due to my experience, I was assigned as the unit instructor pilot and training officer. This job only involved the aircraft type we flew as scouts, the OH-6A Cayuse Light Observation Helicopter. Later I became one of the two Specialized Instructor Pilots for the 101st Airborne Division on the OH-6A.

I gave each scout pilot already assigned to our platoon frequent retraining on both standard and emergency procedures. Whenever possible, I also gave each of our gunners enough instruction so that, if necessary, it would be possible for the gunner to fly the ship in a reasonably straight line. Although it wouldn't look perfect, he could also hover and land without hurting themselves too much. This was, of course, assuming he could somehow get from the back seat to the front cockpit controls quickly enough. It had worked well in Brian's case.

On those occasions when a new pilot decided to become a scout, I put them through the following program:

1. Ten hours of basic flight training in a scout ship. This training was confined to our main base and the local area where, usually, it was relatively safe.
2. Ten hours of flight instruction with the new pilot riding as my gunner. This gave them an opportunity to learn procedures required in combat. They also gained an appreciation for how it felt to be in the back seat with no control.
3. If they passed phase two and desired to continue training, I rode as their gunner while they flew for a total of another ten hours on actual missions. In this case, seniority ruled. I refused to ride in the back seat. I sat forward in the co-pilot's seat near the other controls. I might be crazy, but not totally stupid.

I hated part three. Just as some doctors are the worst patients, I was, am, and always will be the planet's worst passenger. I tried hard not to convey that to the new pilots, but I sometimes think that the churning noises my stomach made prior to those missions may have given my true feelings away.

Knowing that my students were as nervous as I was, I usually tried to lighten things up a bit. I would regal them with any jokes that I had recently heard during the trip en route to our mission and the return. Most seemed at least to appreciate my attempt to put some humor into the situation.

Andy was my only student who did not appreciate it. He bluntly told me to shut up and let him concentrate.

Andy was a strange duck. Not as strange as Weird Bob but not as almost normal as Steve. Andy rarely spoke to anyone, spending most of his spare time alone in his room. At the same time, unlike some other people, he didn't empty his pistol through the door if you happened to knock and invite him out for a game of cards. He even ate alone. If anyone sat down next to him in the mess hall, he moved to another table.

On the other hand, whenever I told him it was time for a training session, Andy was always ready. He loved to fly.

Andy fit right in. He was one of us from his first day. He showed great potential to be a scout pilot.

Andy and I were just completing the third part of his training. As usual, I was up front in the co-pilot's seat performing the gunner's function. We were returning to base after finishing his last mission and required thirty hours of training. Soon, upon landing, I would sign him off as a qualified scout pilot.

But there was one small problem that bothered me. Not once during our twenty hours of actual combat missions did Andy ever have a shot fired in anger at him. I had always been with him and always each job had been more than routine. I was beginning to think this guy was pretty darn lucky.

Bill had even mentioned considering asking if he could rub Andy's balding head for good luck before his missions with me. He quickly gave up that idea. "He'd probably shoot me," Bill said. He was probably right.

While still en route to main base on Andy's last training flight, I checked my flight charts. We were positioned about halfway between the A Shau Valley and our base. About then I decided I should, as an instructor, find out how Andy might react if he came under enemy fire. I believed that, in good faith, I shouldn't complete his training unless I knew if he would accept it calmly or freak out. I also owed it to the gunners who would ride with him in the back seat. We had to know.

My plan to find out was simple yet effective. I pretended to yawn and stretch my arms. As my right arm reached up, I pulled out the overhead circuit breaker that provided power to Andy's side of the radios. With the breaker out, Andy could not hear or talk on his ship-to-ship radio.

However, I could talk and hear on my side of the aircraft. I used the floor button next to my right boot to contact the Cobras that were covering us. Andy had no idea I was broadcasting.

"Hello, 26, this is 14," I called.

"Go ahead 14," I heard in response.

I told the Snakes that I had a problem with the fact that Andy had never been fired on in combat. I asked the lead Cobra to wait two minutes and then excitedly inform Andy that he was receiving enemy fire from his seven o'clock position. The two minutes would give me time to push Andy's radio circuit breaker back in and also pull the breaker that would turn off the power to our mini-gun.

Lead said, "Good idea, 14. We never mentioned it, but we wondered what he'd do. You have two minutes."

My right hand was still up near the overhead panel. Andy still didn't realize what I was doing as I returned power to his radio system by pushing in the breaker. I then pulled the circuit breaker cutting power to our guns. Or at least I thought I had pulled it all the way out. I hadn't. Somehow, as I was soon to discover, it was still making some contact. There was still power. Our guns were operational.

Almost exactly two minutes later, over both our radios, Andy and I heard, "19, you're taking small arms fire from your 7!"

Andy's face showed no surprise. He pulled the ship's nose up, rolled right and entered an attack dive. I turned to look forward and, as an instructor, considered the maneuver he had initiated to be later critiqued at base camp.

From the corner of my eye, I saw his finger begin to depress the trigger to the mini-gun. I could feel a little smile begin to grow on my face, waiting to become a laugh when the guns didn't function.

My smile disappeared as the roar of our mini-gun blasted away just feet from my left side. If it hadn't been for my shoulder harness I have little doubt that I would have hit the overhead window.

I yelled as loud as possible, "Stop! Stop, Andy!" I was just plain yelling while also pushing both the floor radio button and the switch on the co-pilot's stick between my legs.

"Stop it! Stop it!" I hollered.

Andy had become mesmerized by his first personal engagement with the enemy. He wasn't about to listen to anybody.

He continued firing at an enemy force that didn't exist. He did not concern himself with how little mini-gun ammo our ship carried. In seconds, our guns fell silent. It had all been expended on one long pass. At 3,000 rounds a minute, it didn't take long.

He pulled out of his gun run just above the trees, performed another nose-up turn, kicked hard right, and engaged again.

I grabbed the co-pilot's cyclic and shook it. This was a procedure ingrained in all students from the first day of flight school to release control to the instructor.

Andy wouldn't release control. He was stronger than I was. I could not force the aircraft controls.

As he again began his attack, I noticed his finger again pressing the trigger to fire the mini-gun. Instead of a roar, all I heard now was six barrels of our overheated deadly weapon whirling in rotation in the breeze. It only clicked, having no ammo to feed it.

Prior to our takeoff, I had been reading that day's issue of *Stars and Stripes*. I had rolled it up and secured it with one of the rubber bands we kept in the ship. Rubber bands were used to keep the igniting handles on smoke grenades in position in the ship after the pins were pulled. We didn't always have time to pull the pin. We had to prepare. The fall out the ship always broke the rubber band after the grenade was thrown. In any case, I had shoved the rolled up and bound newspaper between my co-pilot's seat and side console so it wouldn't be a problem in flight. I grabbed the newspaper and smacked Andy in the left side of his helmet.

I saw his glazed eyes as his head turned toward me. "What?" he asked.

Before I could explain that we had just been through a training exercise, automatic weapons fire from the ground pierced our helicopter. Tracers, red tracers, whizzed past us. Andy released the controls. Treetop in altitude I took command and rolled hard left. I heard a shaken Cobra pilot's call, "Hey, 19, you really are taking fire!"

"26," I called, "don't cover us, don't shoot!"

I had spent a great deal of time being shot at while performing scout missions. I knew the difference in the sound of an enemy weapon when it fired and one of our weapons. I also knew very well that the enemy used green tracers. These tracers were red. Our forces used red tracers.

We were being fired on by friendly forces.

On my order, and without further incident, our team moved away from the area. We had to sort everything out.

When everyone backed off, I told the Cobras we had been fired on by US manufactured M-16s. Sometimes the enemy used them, but, under heavy fire, as in this case, I could always distinguish the sound of at least some Russian AK-47s.

Not today. All I heard were M-16s. That bothered me.

Andy sat there looking at me and wondering what had happened. The story became clearer to him as he listened to my radio conversation with the Cobra's pilot. When he realized that we had tried to fool him, his look of wonder became a stare and soon, a piercing stare aimed at me.

The Snakes knew the area very well. They had been told no friendly troops were near. They frantically rechecked their maps and our position. The area was clear. No friendly troops, they said. "What was going on?"

Moments later the Cobras received a radio call from HQ that explained everything.

Four days earlier two platoons of South Vietnamese Army troops had been flown into a LZ ten miles from where we were then. During a brief firefight with the enemy, many allied troops had become separated from their command center. The stragglers later met up and, on their own, attempted to reach our lines. Disoriented, they decided to maintain radio silence until they met US forces.

They met US forces. They met us. Accidentally.

Assuming they had an idea who might be there, HQ gave the Cobras the radio frequency of the missing South Vietnamese Army unit.

The Cobras made radio contact. It was them.

In broken Vietnamese, we apologized.

In broken English, they apologized.

They were given their present position coordinates. My overhead cover pilots directed them toward the nearest LZ for pickup and wished them luck. "Before we go, sorry we shot your little helicopter," their ground sergeant radioed.

"No sweat," my lead called back while Andy and I listened. "I understand he was only hit three or four times. For a scout that's a good day."

"Is your small helicopter hearing us?" the South Vietnamese soldier asked.

"I think so. Ask him," lead called. "I believe he hears you."

"Next time," the sergeant said slowly, "that you shoot at me, my American friend, you will join me here in the jungle." He sounded like a person who kept his promises. I didn't care to answer.

Thank goodness nobody got hurt.

I didn't make any friends this day, I thought.

With a wave of my right hand, I indicated to Andy that he had control of the aircraft.

No sooner had we landed at base than I got another radio call, "14, come on up to the hill." It didn't take an identification number to know who was calling me. I knew his voice. It was our CO.

Andy was just shutting down our aircraft after parking it in the protective revetment. I was still sitting in my armored co-pilot seat when Andy jumped out his side door, removed his steel chest plate, and walked around our aircraft to my side. I was ready for a fight. Instead, he extended his hand. Watching his left hand, I shook his right hand.

"You may not believe this, but I understand what you made happen today. You, the team, even me, none of us knew what I'd do in real combat. You gave me a chance to prove myself in a pretend situation. That situation became real."

"I did just what I was trained to do," he continued, "and what I thought I wanted to do. I attacked. My purpose was to kill. I didn't care that you wanted the controls back. I heard you say 'stop' but I didn't care. I couldn't stop pulling the trigger. I was blind with a desire to do the job that was expected of me."

Andy, still shaking my hand, said, "I'll never be able to do it again. Once is enough. I don't care what the circumstances are. I think I'm a good pilot, but now I know I'm not right for this job. Please transfer me."

As Andy and I spoke together that day on the flight line, he confessed that he had always been a stand-off during flight school. He could never decide in his own mind what mission was suited for him. Most new pilots flew Hueys. He wanted more. Or his family wanted more from him.

He came from a military family. He was expected to serve with honor and return with honor. He hadn't ranked high enough in his graduating flight class to attend the prized Chinook or Cobra aircraft training courses. To prove himself to his family, he decided the only option was to volunteer as a 'scout'. He thought that would please them. Our experience together, our experiment together one might say, had opened his mind.

Scouts were great and he respected us. However, he decided, saving lives, not taking lives, was where the real heroes were. He wanted to fly medivacs. His family would never understand. He had to follow his heart as I had followed mine. I agreed. So be it.

I thanked Andy for at least attempting to be a scout. I told him to collect his gear while I arranged his transfer with our CO. I'd see him soon. I had, after all, been ordered to report to him.

Andy went his way. I went mine.

About fifteen minutes later, after brushing my teeth and hair and changing uniforms, I walked toward the CO's office. Before I walked in the door, I saw two Snake pilots standing about ten feet away down the walkway. They each put the first fingers of each hand up to form the sign of a cross. It was a sign of warning. It was also a sign for fighting off evil. I didn't stop to ask which one they meant.

Before I could knock on the CO's door, his smart-mouthed clerk said, "Forget it, he's in his room."

"In his room? It's only 2:30 in the afternoon," I answered.

"Let me clue you in, lieutenant. Number one, he's the boss. His day starts or ends when he says it does. Number two, he may be the boss, but I make this place function. You pilots are nothing. I run this place, without me . . . etc., etc. . . . !"

"Thanks," I said turning away and walking toward the CO's hootch. Arriving, I straightened my jacket and knocked on his door twice.

Nothing.

I pounded twice more, louder.

"Come in, John. Come in."

I opened the door, stepped into his room and, thinking I was in trouble, came to attention. I saluted.

Nobody was in front of where I stood. I looked to my right.

I found myself saluting a man dressed in nothing more than a pair of green boxer shorts. Wagner played over the commander's stereo. At the table next to where our CO was sitting, I saw an inflatable female doll. A physically correct female doll. A physically correct female doll with no clothes on and "Rosie" embossed across her chest.

The commander just waved away my salute. "Sit down. We were just having coffee. Relax."

"We?" I asked.

"Get a grip, lieutenant. My wife, a very open-minded person I might add, decided that if I were to ever have certain 'urges', I should address those urges toward something that reminded me of her. She went shopping at a specialty store, found Rosie and mailed her to me. Whenever I think of my wife, I take time out to role-play a little.

"When I was back in the 'world', I would take off from work every afternoon, go home and have 'high tea' with my wife. I always worked long hours. It was the only time she would truly know I'd be home. Together we'd have our tea and listen to the concert music we love. Then I'd go back to work until late at night. She sent me Rosie so I could stay in touch with reality. Odd, isn't it? Pretending so as to grasp reality," he said.

I thought it might be a good idea just to step backward out the door.

Before I could, my CO said, "So, John, what's this I hear about you and a student trying to fight the war for both sides?"

"Well, sir, it was like this, I was—"

Pleasantly, he cut me short. "Never mind all that. Your Cobra pals already pleaded your case. Consider yourself reprimanded for trying to do the right thing. All charges are dropped," he stated with much waving of arms. "Now, please leave Rosie and me alone."

"Sir?" I questioned.

"Leave, go away, out the door, see you later, bye-bye," he said.

I had just walked out his door when behind me the water kettle on his little butane stove came to a boil and began to whistle. Without mentioning names, I heard someone ask someone else if "she" wanted cream or sugar.

Once again I felt blessed having Patti so near.

# Chapter 5

Fortunately, the resident Snake pilots were more humane to their new additions. They were usually happy to be with us and normally decided to stick it out. Whenever new Snake pilots arrived, I went over to their barracks and introduced myself.

One day I met with a pleasant surprise. There were two more new Snake pilots. While one of the two had just completed Cobra training, the other pilot, Phil, like me, was on his second tour in Vietnam. For whatever reason, he and I had an instant bond.

Later that evening we all met at the Officers Club. Then I discovered Phil and I had more in common than just prior combat experience. He had married an army nurse back in the States. They had come to Vietnam together and she was at the 85th where Patti was stationed.

Now I had someone to share my evening ride to Phu Bai and the early morning flight back to base. The next night after completing our missions, Phil and I flew over to the 85th together for the first time.

I explained on the way that I had to stay in "other available accommodations" since there were those in control who did not consider that Patti and I were married by government standards. He laughed. He didn't have that problem!

As usual, Patti was waiting. This time she, too, had a new friend with her. Barbara, Phil's wife, was by her side. This was great. Men getting off work. Wives greeting them. Just like the real world. If I had a dog and a newspaper I could have shut my eyes and imagined I was home. Unfortunately, I hadn't seen a newspaper since I'd read the paper I'd smacked Andy with, and out here the people ate dogs.

Phil and I were teamed up on several occasions. Twice while he covered me, I was on the receiving end of enemy small-weapons fire. His ability to protect me was awe inspiring, close in and accurate. I hated new Snake drivers whose support fire was either so far away that it was useless or so close that I was hit by the shrapnel from their cannons. Phil did his job very, very well. Also, he was calm on the radio under fire. This greatly compensated for my sometimes screaming and yelling. He was a pleasure to know both on the job and off. He was a friend.

When we lost him, I swore that I would not make any more friends in this place. The agony of losing Phil was worse than the loss of others I had known. Except for Patti, I tried to keep that vow. I failed, but I tried.

Phil was on a mission just inside Vietnam on the Laotian border. His scout was down on the trees. In an instant, an enemy 51 cal. machine gun opened up on Phil. It had been a long burst but Phil, as he told his scout on the radio, thought his ship had been hit only once. The scout came up to Phil's altitude and they headed toward base.

This mission was one of the few during my tour that was flown without a command-in-control rescue helicopter as a part of the team. It was definitely the last.

Suddenly, Phil had problems with his ship. He elected to put it down and wait to be rescued. While his scout ship covered him, he transmitted his mayday. As he made his approach to a level spot in the valley, enemy small-arms fire burst from all directions. The scout engaged the enemy. He wasn't hit, but he was totally overwhelmed by the intense return fire. He had to break his contact.

Meanwhile, Phil and his damaged aircraft were committed to a landing and he had to continue his approach. Another hunter/killer team had heard the "mayday" and was rushing to the scene. Fifteen minutes later the second team and Phil's scout pilot were able to join forces. Together, they went down to access the situation.

It was a mess. Phil's Cobra was burning in the forward ammo compartments. Both front and aft pilot's canopies were open. In the front seat, the pilot/gunner was slumped forward, flames leaping all around him. Phil's seat was empty.

The enemy pulled back. As the ground fire dropped off, our ships began making fast low passes trying to locate Phil. Maybe he was wounded and hiding. He *had* to be there! "Blues," our own unit special infantry assault team, had been launched from our base to the scene via Huey transport helicopter. They were to be dropped in to secure the area.

The first ships on station continued to search and waited for support. They seemed unwilling to consider one more possibility: Phil could have been taken prisoner.

At our base the scream of sirens going on then off in series announced again that one of our own aircraft was down. I was called to head out. Our team was to serve as relief for the other ships on station or already on the way to the crash site. By the time we took off, the Blues were landing.

Radio messages were relayed from the ground after the initial Blues were landed to the Cobras circling the area. These reports were sent to base. En route, we all listened.

After a brief firefight, the Blues set up a defensive perimeter. As additional teams landed, each was sent out to find Phil.

As I arrived, I heard the ground commander radio his report. "We found him."

We can only try to reconstruct what had happened. It appeared that he had left his ship with only a few cuts and scratches even though his aircraft had been hit repeatedly by automatic weapons fire on approach. After getting out of his seat, Phil had lifted the front pilot's canopy to rescue him. He must have realized then that the other pilot was dead. From the many muddy prints of Vietnamese sandals circling the downed helicopter, it appeared as if Phil must have been captured then, almost immediately. Even as the hunter/killer team who responded to the mayday gathered with Phil's scout, he had been led off into the jungle.

I will never understand what happened next. After tying Phil's hands behind his back, they beheaded him.

I went almost crazy with rage as I listened to the radio report.

It may have been naive on my part, but I had always felt a sense of fair play with the North Vietnamese Army regulars. They did their job, for whatever their reason. I did mine. When my tour of duty was done, I would go home. Those guys would be here forever.

With the news of Phil's horrible death, I changed.

I was consumed with sorrow and a maniacal fury.

This war ceased to be a game of cat and mouse. It became a personal battle, and I had a desire to kill.

Command decided to salvage Phil's aircraft. The Blues were told to hold the area until the next day. It was already getting dark.

Phil's body and that of his co-pilot were lifted out shortly after they had been found. I was ordered to accompany the aircraft that took them back to base. I thought of Barbara. How could we ever explain to her what had happened?

To the American mind, there is something unfathomable, terrifying, and somehow evil about a person being beheaded. We could not allow her to discover the truth.

I radioed the other ship and asked to meet the aircraft commander after landing at the unit base.

We met and after a short conversation, we both went to see our commanding officer.

We explained how terrible it was going to be to tell Barbara that Phil was dead. To tell her how he had died would be unbearable for her and devastating to us.

We had thought it all through and decided to switch the name tags on the body bags. If Barbara demanded to see Phil's body, as we thought she would, she'd see a burned and unrecognizable body. The co-pilot. Not Phil.

We would take Phil's wedding ring, which was unique, and place it on the other body. It would be returned where it belonged later. We would also return the name tags later.

We all knew that eventually the bodies would be sealed in metal caskets and marked "Not for Viewing." By then it would be all over.

Our CO didn't like the idea or any part of it. He would not authorize it. He had never heard of it, but for Barbara's sake we should do it.

We did.

Barbara had been told Phil was gone and had been given a light sedative. Patti was on duty in surgery and could not be with her. When we arrived, Barbara and all those who could be there were waiting.

She immediately asked to see him. We told her about the burns. She brushed our words aside. The bag was unzipped. She saw the ring and that was enough. She knew Phil was truly gone.

Without a word, she turned and walked away. That night she was sent to Saigon. Two days later she and another officer escorted Phil's casket back to his home.

Although Patti and I have never seen or heard from Barbara again, she and Phil are never far from our hearts or minds.

In retrospect, I do not know if what we did was right or moral. I can only hope that, because of our deception, Barbara found less grief than what the truth held.

The next morning I flew back to the area of the downed ship to help provide security for the infantry. During the night there had been several contacts with the enemy. None of the combat had been sustained for any length of time, but there were casualties on both sides.

Two of our troopers were wounded. Several enemy bodies were found, plus a couple of bloody trails left by injured enemy soldiers.

Remarkably, a wounded NVA officer had been taken prisoner. Although shot in both legs, he would live.

He was brought out with our infantry when the salvage mission of Phil's aircraft was abandoned due to the enemy presence. His ship was simply blown in place and all personnel were extracted. It would have been foolish to risk more casualties for nothing more than a now worthless mass of twisted burnt metal.

My next day's flights had been canceled so, in the late morning, I took my scout ship over to see Patti. She was in the emergency room.

On two of the tables lay troopers who had been wounded the night before and extracted that morning. Doctors and nurses hovered over them.

Patti stood by the third table preparing a prone figure for surgery. Standing a few steps away was Weird Bob—frozen, unmoving, glaring. As I came closer, I saw what he was staring at. It was the wounded NVA officer.

Bob felt my presence. Turning to me, he whispered, "You know, man, maybe he's the one who gave the order! Maybe he's the one who killed Phil!"

My hand reached slowly for my pistol, as the fire of my hate burned hot.

The wounded officer, eyes cold, stared at me uncaring. As my palm touched my weapon, I heard a sudden, *"No!"*

*"No!"* Patti yelled again. "Not here! Not ever here! You leave your lousy war outside . . . you and all the others with your killing and maiming. This is not your arena. Here we fight to save people. All people! There's enough death outside! Now, go! *Go!*"

I walked out the door and sat down on a wooden bench. I had a lot of soul-searching to do.

Bob followed and then stopped. He looked me in the eye and shook his head. "You're losing your edge, man," he said. "Be careful." He was stunned that I hadn't pulled the trigger.

I met Patti later when she was off duty. I apologized for what had happened.

"You have to understand and accept what I do," she said. "None of this is easy for me either. My stress and confusion may be different from yours but they are certainly not less. I grieve too. There are so many people who need help—always more. I have to put the hurt behind me and go on with business as usual. You have to let go of your hate or it will consume you. Not only you but us as well."

I would try, I thought. It would take time, but I would try.

As in any war, there are stories that are horrid and stories that are strange. This story meets both qualifications. I have neither tried to interpret what happened nor have I added to the story of this particular mission. I was only a minor player. I am writing about what I remember from the afternoon reports and what was told to me by those who survived.

A ranger unit was inserted into the A Shau Valley jungle by our sister unit, C troop, 2nd Squadron, 17th Cavalry. This ranger unit was to monitor enemy movement and, if necessary, engage the enemy. Soon after being inserted, they discovered a trail that had been traveled by six to eight enemy troops about one to two hours earlier.

The ranger unit decided to continue moving and link up with another ranger platoon already in the area. Together, they were to set up a security position just outside the nearest suitable helicopter landing zone.

Both units were well within territory held in full control by North Vietnamese troops.

Just before the ranger units managed to join together, there was a brief fire fight between one of the US units and enemy forces. One American was killed.

After joining forces, one of the two US platoons sent a squad to recover the body of the dead ranger. They strapped the body into a harness called a McGuire Rig. These harnesses were often used to extract our killed or wounded from areas where helicopters could not land.

The helicopter and crew given the mission would approach the area, hover overhead, drop a long line hooked to the harness attached to the dead or wounded, then begin bringing up the long line by hand as the ship departed—quickly and often under fire.

The enemy, knowing we Americans always, *always* made every effort to recover our injured and killed, waited for just such opportunities.

During this mission, the enemy had many opportunities. They took advantage of every one.

A helicopter flew to the ranger unit, hovered over the jungle and the dead trooper, dropped its line and waited for him to be attached. That part of the mission completed, the aircraft began to depart. Suddenly it came under intense hostile small arms fire from several directions.

There was a heavy hunter/killer team, two Cobras plus one scout, in the area. The scout engaged the enemy, firing on muzzle flashes because the pilot could not see individual enemy troops. The Cobras covering the scout could not protect their recon ship for fear of hitting our own troops on the ground.

Under covering fire from the scout ship, the rangers sent to recover their dead trooper were able to return to their platoon.

Short of fuel, the aircraft departed. Others were on their way.

After a short time, one of the two ranger platoon leaders looked to his northeast. From his position he saw about thirty heavily armed enemy soldiers about a hundred feet away standing in a small open area in groups of four or five. They showed no fear. Having no allied aircraft overhead made them even braver. All enemy soldiers were carrying automatic weapons.

Within minutes, our two ranger platoons began receiving rocket propelled grenades on their position. Enemy fire was from as near as thirty feet.

The enemy was close. Very close.

There were reports of hand-to-hand combat.

Then something happened that surprised all the American Rangers. It shocked their officers to the point of ordering everyone to hold their fire.

The enemy platoon leader stood and began giving his orders to his troops in English.

It was not, to those who heard, the accent of a Vietnamese educated in the United States or England.

It was an American speaking English with an American accent.

Among other orders that were given, our rangers heard, "Get that RPG (rocket propelled grenade) over here!" and "Move!" "Fire!" The enemy always seemed to understand and follow all orders.

The next hunter/killer team arrived. The team was informed of the enemy orders being given in English.

Once again the Cobras could not engage. Only the scout, being face to face with the enemy, could fire on the enemy so close to the ranger perimeter.

The enemy, knowing the scout could not engage after passing overhead, closed in. The Cobras continued to hold fire. Their rockets were too powerful to allow impact so close to our own troops.

More orders were heard in English, "Move—you—yes, you! Fire—fire!"

The battle lasted less than twenty minutes.

The enemy did not pull back. They simply ceased fire and waited.

For a moment, a lifetime to some, it was quiet.

A short distance away, many more American troops were flown in by helicopter. A little late. A little too far away.

Just because our reinforcements were near, the enemy didn't seem impressed.

So far the body count was one American killed, four wounded. Enemy unknown.

Later that afternoon, another ranger team was inserted with scout ships into a LZ closer to the original ground unit.

The LZ was small. For this reason scout aircraft would bring in troops. It was one aircraft in and out, the next one landing. I was part of the insertion team.

The first ship in had a trooper on board wounded immediately. He was flown out without ever leaving the ship. The second scout landed and dropped off its three troops. Even without gunners aboard, we could only carry three heavy US troops and their gear. The third ship, a Huey, thinking the LZ looked large enough for him to land, was shot down on final approach. The pilot, knowing the importance of keeping the LZ open, purposely crashed into the trees. His eight troops on board escaped unhurt. Two stayed to protect him while the others joined the ranger team.

We scouts managed to bring in three more loads of troops, always three troops to a ship.

The Huey pilot who thought he could land in the tight LZ had attempted to land more troops than we scouts could in several trips. Now his co-pilot and one gunner were dead. He was badly wounded. His other gunner was injured and hiding in the bush. The two rangers who stayed with him were killed in a brief firefight. As night fell, one volunteer ranger from the main unit returned to the downed helicopter. He found the gunner that was hiding in the jungle. They lay down as flat as possible. The ranger covered them both with brush to camouflage themselves. Believing nobody else could have survived the crash, he didn't return to the downed aircraft.

He was wrong.

That night our entire squadron—pilots, gunners, observers, cooks, medics, truck drivers, everyone—sat crowded together but silent in our radio room waiting for any and all reports.

We listened to a frightening story.

The Air Force was over the various positions as were our night-equipped Cobras. Again, the enemy was too close. They couldn't do much but wait until daylight.

The Air Force did one thing for us that night, though. It was a duty fate found they had to accomplish. In the end, they wished it were combat.

The pilot from the downed Huey who, knowing he was shot down and, to keep the LZ clear for our other ships, had crashed into the trees, was still alive.

He was trapped in the cockpit. His console was pressed against his chest. His legs were pinned by other wreckage.

However, he still had his helmet on and his radio worked.

The Air Force relayed his softly spoken messages. Through them we heard, from our downed pilot, call sign "32": "32 says the enemy is in the back of his ship." "32 says he thinks they're playing cards." Later, "he says they're smoking pot." Still later, "32 says they must not want to give away their position by firing a weapon. They're using a dead helicopter crewman for bayonet practice."

I could almost feel the warm stains of tears rolling down the Air Force pilot's cheeks as he choked out the words.

It wasn't long before I realized the tears were also mine.

It was a long night. Around 2 A.M., 32's radio stopped transmitting.

By 3 A.M. and a short briefing, our next day's plan was complete.

Reinforce.

Just before dawn, three heavy hunter/killer teams were released from the chains of darkness to attack. Orders: Secure the crash site; prepare the surrounding area for massive troop arrival.

Weird Bob got the difficult job. He was to be the first in. They didn't even ask him; they knew they didn't have to. He was to fly two Special Forces troops and one of their medics into the LZ nearest the downed Huey.

The rest of us would attempt to put troops in behind him. Again, one ship in and out, the next ship in. No ships larger than a scout aircraft.

All Weird Bob said was, "You know, I hoped they'd volunteer me."

As the sun rose over the jungle canopy, Bob landed in the LZ. His passengers were out the doors and running for cover before he touched down. Up and out he flew.

The enemy let us know they were still there.

The next scout behind Bob was shot down. Paul, the pilot, managed to touch down level as his troopers exited. Paul's ship, hit, rolled down slope as his engine caught fire, clearing the LZ for the rest of us. Paul, somehow unhurt, joined the SF troops at the downed Huey.

Although still under fire, we continued to drop in special troops. As our troops gained control heavier aircraft used another larger LZ nearby to insert more forces.

Another ship went down. Then another. Still our helicopters arrived.

Many were wounded. A few killed.

The area began to swarm with American troops. Our men proceeded first to our LZ and the Huey. Saving the brave trapped pilot was foremost in everyone's mind. When the second wave of troops arrived at "32's" position, they assisted the Special Forces in pushing back the enemy force that remained in the area.

The SF medic never stopped doing what he could to keep "32" alive.

An unusual radio was heard. The medic with "32" needed another scalpel to cut "32" free. His first one was now too dull. A command ship dropped another full medical kit.

Both of "32's" legs were amputated on site before he could be flown out to a hospital. The 85th.

It took all day for all of our units to finally fight their way through small pockets of enemy resistance and linkup. That night the enemy did nothing more than harass our troops.

No further commands were ever heard in English given by the enemy officers.

The next morning, all our forces were loaded up and flown out with few, if any problems from the enemy.

When our withdrawal was complete, I returned to main base and refueled and rearmed. The CO gave me permission to fly over to Patti's unit where "32" was hospitalized. He asked me to take some of his friends with me. I carried as many as I could lift. More were behind me in another ship.

I radioed ahead. Patti met us at the helipad. "32" was in intensive care just past the emergency room's large twin doors.

"He doesn't have much time," she said in a matter-of-fact voice. "Just a few of you at a time and then even a couple of seconds each. Remember, he needs your strength, not your pity. If you can't give him that, don't go in there."

We tried. It wasn't easy.

The third group of his friends had just walked in when "32" just seemed to go to sleep.

He was gone.

When everyone else had left, Patti looked at me, shook her head, and walked away. Alone, I slept that night under my aircraft, dreaming of a peach farm many miles away.

✦ ✦ ✦

A few days later Patti heard something that no doubt made her wonder whether I would ever conquer my loathing of the enemy.

During a reconnaissance mission over a small river valley, I surprised ten North Vietnamese soldiers, weapons over their heads, crossing a chest deep stream. Following reflex motion, I opened fire with my mini-gun. My gunner also engaged them simultaneously.

They never had a chance. They didn't fire a single round. In seconds, the stream ran red with the blood of ten unmoving bodies.

I was elated.

When we returned to base, I went straight to the CO's room. I was so excited about what I had done that I wanted to tell him about it right away.

I knocked and walked in. "Guess who . . . ," he started to say.

I didn't give him a chance to finish. I proceeded to give him all the details in vivid technicolor.

When I finished, he looked slowly off to my right and pointed. There sat Patti with two other nurses. They had all come over for a visit.

Patti's eyes were filled with questions. Is this the man I love? Or is this someone I have never met?

As I looked at her, I thought not only about what I had said but also how I had told the story so proudly. I knew then that I had compromised all that was truly important to me.

My hate, my need for revenge all drained away. While this war would never go back to being a game, it could never again be a personal vendetta. It was a job. Just a job. Nothing more. Nothing less.

Patti and I talked at length that night.

I often wonder what I would have become if I had not had Patti's strength and faith in us from which to draw.

# Chapter 6

In the weeks that followed the death of Phil and "32," the rumor mill began spreading a strange tale about the enemy. The story involved the Vietnamese strong belief in many superstitions and their particular fear of the ace of spades from an ordinary deck of cards. It represented death to them. The story was that the NVA even avoided jungle trails that had been marked with this card. It was also said that if you wore an ace of spades on your uniform, the enemy would leave you alone if they were close enough to see it.

Within hours there wasn't a full poker deck in our camp.

The same evening I heard this story I wrote a letter to a fellow pilot with whom I had gone to flight school. Although he was "down south," he, too, was with a calvary unit, so I tolerated him. I jokingly mentioned the bit about the ace.

A week later I got a package back from him. Inside were two decks of cards and a note. He explained that they had heard the story sometime before and that there was little if any truth in it. It was, however, effective in another way. Morale improved when the men had the good fortune to carry the black ace. Nobody went out and played like they were John Wayne because of a "dumb old card," but they

did feel better when doing their jobs. Their unit CO had
gone so far as to order poker decks from a major manufac-
turer that contained nothing but the ace of spades. He had
enclosed two decks.

"Try it," he wrote.

I did.

I went over to the enlisted men's hootch, knocked on
the door and announced myself. I had learned that no matter how close I might think I was to my men, I was still an
officer. That bar on my collar made me different. Not better, just different.

Their hootch, just like mine, represented a little piece
of private space. It was a special spot where we could be
among our own "things" and think an occasional good
thought. Unless it was necessary, I did not like to infringe
on the few moments that they had to be individuals.

Surprises were not always welcome. Having an officer
around was not what they considered a relaxing moment.
Besides these reasons to let them know I was around, there
was one more. They might be doing something I didn't want
to know about. To save any problems, paperwork and an
outside chance of getting my head blown off, I had learned
to knock. It was better for all concerned.

Once inside I announced in a solemn voice, "I have a
gift for you." To each trooper I presented an ace of spades.

When I started, I heard a couple of guys behind me ask,
"What's he doing? What's he handing out?"

Then a muffled shout. "It's the ace!"

Nobody was truly fooled. They knew this whole card
business wasn't for real but maybe, just maybe, it might work.

In the end, they appreciated the cards and I was glad to
have been able to give them each one. Morale did go up.

As a group, they began to police the area. When some of them even trimmed their sideburns and mustaches, the CO mumbled something about the platoon "looking up." He had never made that statement before. When I asked him to repeat it, thinking I had heard him wrong, he just shrugged and kept walking.

Unfortunately it was only a fad and, like all fads, it wore out in time. For a while, though, a simple thing like a poker card provided a little bit of magic and security, however slight.

To this day, mine is tucked safely in my wallet.

✦  ✦  ✦

Soon after this we were ordered to conduct a mission into the Laotian Salient. This was an area well west of the A Shau Valley. I had never been there before and was somewhat apprehensive about being that far into enemy territory.

We had much more flight planning than usual. Actually, to be truthful, our commanders did most of the planning for us but it sounds good to say we pilots had an opportunity to talk to someone about it before it happened. Regardless, the planning worked. Refueling and rearming depots were put in position and well placed.

We flew from Vietnam, over the A Shau and into Laos. We landed when necessary and, without shutting down our engines, took on fuel and whatever ammo was needed. There were no problems. Strangely, I learned years later this was all accomplished within fifteen miles of one of the enemy's largest known bases and training facilities outside of North Vietnam. I guess someone decided that if they could do it to us, we could do it to them.

I was beginning my third recon mission of the day following our refueling out of large rubber bladders. A heavy- lift helicopter company assigned to the 101st Airborne Division had flown these fuel bladders into position for us.

Intelligence had told us to expect massive enemy resistance. So far there had been nothing, not so much as the backfiring of an enemy truck.

Unlike the mountains I was used to flying, this area was reasonably flat. It was also a very beautiful land. Both Bill and I were impressed.

"Hey, LT?" asked Bill.

"Yeah, what?" I answered.

"Do you think that maybe after this war is over it'll be safe to walk around this place without getting blown up by a stray land mine? This is nice."

"I doubt it," I said. "Please pay attention to business. I've got a gut feeling all of a sudden."

"Take a Rolaids, LT."

The days were short that time of year and the light went quickly in the late afternoon. Our day would be over soon. I'd be back with Patti soon.

About a half-hour into the mission I was flying along a low ridge. It had some rather tall brush along one side and the top. I had decided to check out the ridge because it provided the only serious cover in so much otherwise level territory. I was flying lower than normal due to the lack of anything to hide the aircraft behind if something went wrong.

Both Bill and I had our heads out our respective doors looking around for anything unusual. Then I spotted something. Something white. I informed Bill and called our cover ships.

"What was it?" they asked.

"I'm not sure. Stand by," I replied.

Bill and I looked around the ridge quickly and seeing nothing that we hadn't seen before, hovered cautiously over the white object.

I spoke at the same time as my gunner, "It's a rocket!" "And not one of ours!" I added.

"What kind of rocket?" I was asked.

"A 122 mm," I said. "There's some writing on the side and it's not English. I see some numbers also. Just a second."

We hovered down a bit and a little closer to our right side. We could almost touch it with our skids.

I was reading the numbers over the radio to the Cobras when, out of the corner of my eye, I saw a flash of light reflecting off something shiny. Like a mirror. Or a cannon barrel.

I sat up so fast I smashed the back of my helmet into the overhead doorframe. That's when I saw it. Not more than a hundred feet away was an enemy 37 mm antiaircraft gun. I was close enough to see every detail of it and the crew manning it. They were hand cranking it very, very slowly around to get a point-blank shot at a sitting duck. Us.

When the enemy gunners began moving their large weapon into position to fire and knock us down, the sun, being low, had reflected just enough light off their barrel to startle me into looking up. Fortunately, they weren't quite ready to accomplish their deed when I finally saw them.

Before the enemy gunners could fire, I was moving out, screaming on the radio, pulling the trigger of my mini-gun and trying hard to maneuver behind any blade of tall grass or brush that would have us.

The situation was not good. However, I managed to make the overall problem even worse. Instead of doing as I was trained and report on what was happening, all anyone heard over their radios was a long list of profanities punctuated by bursts from my mini-gun and Bill's M-60 machine gun. I had been too shocked and surprised to keep a clear head.

After we had cleared the area and the Cobras had pretty well expended their ammo at they didn't know what, we climbed up to altitude. By then I had stopped yelling non-sense. Now I went the other way. I could hardly talk.

Bill asked, "LT, what happened?" He hadn't seen the enemy weapon. He had opened fire because I had begun shooting.

All I could say was "37."

"37? 37 what?" Bill questioned.

I took several deep breaths. Get it together, I told myself. I could finally speak. "Didn't you see it? There was a 37 mm antiaircraft gun just at our right door!"

"You're kidding—right?" Bill asked.

"No."

I was ready to call the Snakes and explain what had happened. I wanted them to know that I wasn't sure if we had managed to put the enemy gun crew out of action or not. Considering the type of weapon and its range, every-one might still be in danger.

Before I could say a word, another ship radioed me. "Little Bird, I understand your call sign is Banshee 14?"

I didn't know who was calling and I didn't answer. All I wanted to do was tell our other team members that there were antiaircraft weapons in the area.

I knew I hadn't been professional under fire and had certainly used some four letter words that I regretted. How-ever, it also wasn't normal to interrupt a mission in progress and mention aircraft call signs in the open on certain ra-dios. I knew that the radio I had been called on had been reported as possibly not secure.

The next thing I heard was, "This is the artillery battalion commander. I will not allow anyone, for any reason, to use that language on the radio! I don't care what the problem might be! Do you understand?"

All he got from me was two radio clicks meaning I understood. For a moment the radio was quiet. Then there were two more clicks, but not from me. Then more clicks. More, then more. The airwaves became jammed with double clicks from other ships in our unit that were in the area. There were too many clicks too fast for the artillery commander to believe it was just me being obnoxious. No one person could push one radio button that fast.

The other pilots in the area were showing their solidarity by pushing their buttons in response to my answer. If I got scared once in a while, so be it. I was doing a job they definitely didn't want.

The commander was not impressed. He began yelling over the radio for everyone to stop—now!

While all this was going on, the enemy gunnery crew that I had almost shook hands with earlier and not reported, or been able to report due to the artillery commander being on the radio, began gathering their range data. About the same time the commander finished telling everyone to knock it off, the first *ack-ack* bursts began popping around us.

After years of dealing with our air operations, the enemy knew our procedures well. They knew I was the scout. Above me were the bad boys—the Cobras. A little higher was where the medivac/rescue ships flew. If there were aircraft above them, the enemy knew that they were most likely command ships and ranking officers.

Having regained my composure, I radioed, "Excuse me, sir, but I've been trying to tell you—they have anti-aircraft down there."

As expected, the first bursts targeted us. The next were above us. The next were higher. By the time the *ack-ack* reached the artillery commander, he was using words over the radio I had not used and a few I had never heard before. It seemed he didn't like that gun crew any better than I did.

It was pretty obvious by now that I had not been able to disable the enemy gun crew. Either that or there was more than one.

My lead Snake pilot broke in and ordered our team to another preset radio frequency. We began making evasive turns and rapid altitude changes.

All this time Bill was silent. When he did speak up it was very informative. "Lieutenant," he said, "I know you're busy, but I can see those '37' guys."

"Say that again," I ordered.

"Well," he said, "while we've been up here, I've been checking that ridge we were flying. I can see puffs of smoke from just one weapons crew every time they fire. I don't know if you got one or not but there's only one now."

I radioed the lead Cobra. I explained that Bill could identify the enemy position on the ridge that I had scouted earlier. There seemed to be only one gun emplacement. Our lead gave us two choices of action. The first was just to call in the Air Force and go home. The other was to take the gun out ourselves. What did I want to do?

I didn't like either choice. The enemy might be able to move the weapon before the jets arrived. At least trying to destroy the gun ourselves would give me a chance to redeem myself. The gun wasn't the only problem to deal with though. Weapons of that caliber usually had at least some infantry protection.

I turned around and looked at Bill. He nodded and pointed down.

"OK, lead, let's get him," I called.

When the rocket ships were in position to cover me, I departed altitude.

The enemy anti-aircraft crew was paying too much attention to the other ships to notice us. Flying as fast as possible and approaching from their rear, Bill and I fired our machine guns as we got close. We saw only a few infantry troops. Bill dropped three red smoke grenades as we passed overhead. His accuracy was unbelievable. Looking back behind us, I saw one grenade bounce off the dirt only feet from the gun turret before sending up a cloud of red.

The target was marked.

Besides covering me, my Cobras had been also making a few radio calls. They had returned to the frequency we had been on earlier and requested any other Snakes in the area to join us. Within minutes two teams of Aerial Rocket Artillery (ARA) Cobras were on the scene.

We were used to, and expecting the cover fire from, our Cobras rockets and their 40 mm cannon fire exploding behind us to keep unfriendly heads down. I wasn't told that ARA had arrived and was ready to assist in our cover.

As we cleared the enemy positions and our smoke grenades did their job, Bill and I heard massive explosions off our tail. The concussion from the ARA rockets hit us hard. I began swearing again, this time silently. My lead cover ship told me not to worry, it was friendly fire. "Thank goodness they're on our side," I radioed.

Soon, our own squadron commander arrived overhead and requested an update. After he was filled in, he called me, "Is she knocked out?"

"I hope so," I answered.

"Make sure," he said.

I turned again to Bill. He looked me in the eye and, without a word, slammed the bolt forward on his M-60 machine gun. I knew his answer. I checked my instruments. In my flight controls I could feel Bill's weight shift in the rear seat as he began to reposition himself half in, half out of our tiny helicopter. Looking to my right rear, I saw his feet firmly placed on the aircraft skid.

I stood the ship up on its nose and did a torque turn to reverse our heading. Back we went.

I knew that we were in everyone's gun sights. The gun sights of my cover ships to protect us. The gun sights of the enemy to knock us down.

Once again we approached the target. As we got closer, nothing happened. We overflew the gun position; nothing happened. Not even one round was fired at us. Even Bill, who had what might be called an itchy finger, didn't shoot. Nor did I.

We made four or five passes. All we saw were bodies. There was nobody left to fire on us. ARA had done more damage than I thought.

On what I was considering to be my last fast pass over the target, I was overwhelmed with a strange feeling of security. Immediately over the anti-aircraft emplacement, I completed a "quick stop" maneuver. In seconds we were hovering only two or three feet off the ground and only feet from the enemy weapon.

Out the corner of my eye I saw Bill disconnect his safety harness and throw his flight helmet onto the ship's floor behind him. He jumped out his open door.

I have no idea what I would have done if any enemy troops had been left to open fire on us. We were at a hover. I saw Bill quickly cut the insignia off the uniform collars of two nearby dead enemy soldiers with his survival knife. Running back to our aircraft, he grabbed two NVA weapons along the way and threw them into our back seat. He then merely stepped on the ship's skids and sat back down in his seat. I felt two taps on my shoulder from behind.

Go.

I did.

We climbed to altitude and joined our team. The Cobras led the way home.

Bill and I, hearts pounding, said little on the way back to main base. The Snake pilots didn't say much either. The only thing I remember lead saying was "Hey, man, maybe we should talk tonight."

We arrived at base safely. I shut down the aircraft. Neither Bill nor I moved from our seats for ten or fifteen minutes. We just sat there letting the adrenaline drain from our bodies. Nobody bothered us.

After a while, though, our squadron commander walked up. To Bill he asked, "Got something for me?"

"Yes, sir. Here." He handed him the enemy uniform collar insignias.

"Intelligence will be pleased," the commander said. "You guys can keep the weapons. John, the radio room told me Patti called a couple of times. Why not fly over tonight and take a day off tomorrow?"

To Bill he said, "You come with me. I've got a bottle of brandy in my hootch. We can put rank away for a few hours. Maybe you'll tell me at what age your mother dropped you on your head."

I started up my engine while they walked off together. As I took off toward the 85th Evac and Patti, I saw Bill, about thirty yards away, stop, turn, come to attention and salute me. I returned his salute.

His salute was more of an honor to me than any award
that could ever be pinned to my chest.

Patti was waiting for me on the helipad when I arrived
in Phu Bai. She escorted me to the Officers Club where she
and a few of her friends presented me with a cake.

I'd forgotten. It was my birthday.

I was now officially twenty-two years old.

Please never let it be known that we helicopter pilots
had any respect for jet fighter pilots. We spent a great deal
of energy and time bad-mouthing them behind their backs
and, if there were more of us than them, to their faces.

In reality, we both respected and trusted them. Those
"fast mover" pilots were, and always will be, special. Regardless of their service, Navy, Marine Corps, or Air Force,
our hearts were strengthened when they were on station.
They supported our fire bases, protected infantry units in
combat, and gave any Allied force who requested it their
vengeance against enemy attacks.

We loved having them around. They made us feel
powerful.

However, their power was sometimes fleeting. Because
they took so many risks to keep others alive, their casualty
rates were high.

If we knew a fighter had been hit and gone down, any
recon mission we were involved in ceased. We went to them.
Even though they had their own search and rescue helicopters, we tried our best to be there when needed and
several times our hunter/killer teams were in position to
offer assistance.

Weird Bob was on one such mission. Unfortunately, it was not a mission that ended the way any of us would have ever hoped.

Weird Bob and his cover "rocket" ships had just departed main base when the Cobras received a call that an Air Force observation spotter airplane, an OV-10, had seen many enemy troops in an open area. The area was just east of the A Shau Valley, our operations zone. They headed that direction.

Normally, the Air Force observation propeller airplane would await our arrival if we were not far away. When we got close, they would alert the jets to circle overhead. The scout would go down, assess the situation and mark targets with red smoke. The observation plane would monitor the scout's radio reports and choose what he considered to be the best targets of opportunity. The hunter/killer team would then withdraw a few miles. The "big boys" would take over for awhile.

The observation airplane usually carried six white phosphorous rockets, three on each wing. When the jets were in position, the spotter airplane would mark the targets that were to be struck by the fighters.

Like us, they operated as a team.

The scout ship would return after the strike to conduct a "bomb damage assessment." The results were tallied and everyone went home—usually.

By the time Weird Bob's team arrived on scene this day, the jets had already begun their attacks. The observer had committed the fighter jets because, quite frankly, he didn't need a scout to point out enemy positions. He had been the one to spot the troops in the first place. The hunter/killer team was asked to stand off while he marked his next target with his last rocket. Weird Bob was certainly welcome to do a damage assessment afterward, the observer said.

Weird Bob was frustrated. He didn't like not being more involved. But he, like all of us, loved to watch the jets work out. He was waiting, although not patiently.

The jets began diving on the spotters final marker rocket. They came speeding down from high altitude, released their loads and went almost straight back up to altitude.

While Weird Bob and his team watched, two jets completed their runs. The third entered his dive, let loose his bomb load and initiated his climb.

Tracers came from three different positions from the ground. The third jet seemed to slow its climb and then flutter a bit. Hit by small-arms fire, he flamed out.

The fighter erupted in flames. Weird Bob saw its canopy fly off, followed by a small dark dot and a few seconds later, a small dark dot attached to a parachute.

The pilot had ejected.

We didn't call Weird Bob "Weird Bob" for no reason. He immediately departed formation and began climbing toward the now slowly falling jet pilot. He never told anyone what he was doing. I understood later that Bob's gunner made the only radio call to his team, and he could only speculate on what they were doing.

As the fighter pilot floated to earth, the enemy directed their small arms fire to him. He was unprotected.

Unprotected—except for Weird Bob.

Bob followed him all the way down. Bob did everything he could to draw the enemy fire to himself and his aircraft. Whenever he saw muzzle flashes from the ground, he opened fire with his mini-gun and sprayed the area.

Somehow the jet pilot was able to land in a small clearing. As his parachute unfurled around him, he began to disconnect himself from his harness. Weird Bob was flying low passes close overhead and firing into the surrounding trees trying to cover him.

To their credit, the Air Force already had a huge, very well armed rescue helicopter known as the "Jolly Green Giant" on long approach to the position. As Bob made a tight turn over the clearing, he saw the downed pilot reach for his survival radio. In his other hand he held a pistol. He waved his pistol at Bob and smiled. At that moment, with Bob able to do nothing more than look on, several enemy troops walked out of the tree line edging the clearing and sprayed the smiling, waving pilot with automatic weapons fire. He fell where he stood.

Seeing what happened, Bob tightened his turn even further, almost to the point of slipping his aircraft into the out-reaching limbs of the jungle canopy.

With what ammo was left, Bob and his gunner took revenge on those who had taken the life of a man who, with a wave and a smile, had come as close to becoming Bob's friend as anyone ever would.

Even with no ammunition remaining, Bob refused to leave the area until he was almost run over by the Jolly Green Giant attempting to recover the downed pilot's body.

Knowing there was nothing more he could do, Weird Bob, rather than rejoin the formation and his team, merely headed back to base alone. The Cobras saw what he was doing but had to stay on station until released by command. Their radio calls to Bob went unanswered. His gunner knew better than to say anything more.

When you flew with Weird Bob you were usually just along for the ride.

Steve, Mike, and I were playing poker in the scout hootch when Bob walked in the door. Bob was one of those people who, just by looking into his eyes, you knew it was better to be quiet. This was one of those times.

For two days he stayed in his room. He didn't eat or speak in that time. Nobody even gathered the courage to ask if everything was all right. A few months before, we had knocked on his door to check on him during one of his dark moments and were answered by six rounds from his revolver fired into the floor in front of us. We decided then that it was better to just let him come out when he felt the time was right.

When he did come out on his own, he just walked over, sat down at the table of our seemingly endless ongoing poker game, gently placed his pistol on the table in front of his seat and announced it was his deal.

As one, we all immediately handed him our cards. It was a long and, thankfully, uneventful night.

I seem to remember Bob winning some rather large pots that night. It was safer that way.

✦ ✦ ✦

A few weeks went by and all the necessary pieces for the "real wedding" for Patti and I were coming together. All the paperwork had been completed. Announcements arrived. Ingredients for a cake had been stolen or traded for. The 151st Aviation Chapel had been reserved and the date was pending. Where to go on a honeymoon was decided.

In the meantime, Patti and I spent as much time together as possible and waited.

Finally, in March, the Army sent a message. Permission granted! Set a date! Patience had won out over what we had termed "the green machine." We decided on April 11, 1971.

As the date approached, the first of several tragedies struck. Two pilot friends of ours were inbound to the 85th from a night mission. They had been in the "valley" extracting the survivors of an ambush team that had been overwhelmed by the enemy.

Seven troopers had been picked up. Six were wounded and they were inside the ship. Both the helicopter gunner and the gunner/mechanic were also wounded. Below the ship, strapped to a one-hundred foot line, was another wounded trooper who had been pulled from the jungle on the rope.

Patti and I were on one of our walks and saw the scene unfold as they approached the hospital. Their aircraft simply quit flying; it fell like a rock. We never learned why.

The trooper on the rope struck the ground first. Then the rope that connected him to the helicopter caught on something. It pulled the falling ship further out of control. It exploded on contact.

There was nothing we could do but watch the nightmare unfold. There were no survivors.

A few days later, one of my fellow scout pilots was shot down. He had arranged our wedding invitations through a friend back home. He was hit at 1500 feet altitude while on a mission and spun into the ground. The pilot was killed instantly when his ship was first hit. His gunner in the back seat talked to us all the way down. He was killed on impact.

I had been flying into the area to relieve them on station. Despite heavy enemy fire, I went down to locate survivors. There were none. I was ordered to withdraw.

# Chapter 7

The afternoon of April 10, the day before our wedding, was to have been my bachelor party. Knowing this, my commanding officer, who was to stand in as my father at the ceremony, gave me the day off from flight operations. "Let the boy enjoy his last free day," he told someone. He took what would have been my mission himself.

Somewhere near the Laos border, his ship took several direct hits from a radar controlled anti-aircraft gun. The CO was severely wounded. Although also wounded, his co-pilot managed to get control of the ship and head for the 85th hospital.

Patti was there when they arrived. She and several doctors struggled for hours to keep the CO alive. In the end, they lost him.

That afternoon and evening there was no bachelor party. A different sort of ceremony was held in its place. It's called "Boots and Saddles," a cavalry tribute to fallen comrades.

Later I flew over to see Patti. She must have heard I was coming because she was on the ramp when I arrived.

I spoke first. "Are we doing the right thing? The next mission or the one after that could put me on one of those surgical tables. Would you prefer it to be a friend lying there or your husband?"

Her eyes were tired. "I want to be your wife for life, but if that life is only a day, I'll be happy to have had that long."

Little more was said that night.

✦ ✦ ✦

The next day we all tried to set aside our mourning to celebrate a new joining, a new beginning. A marriage.

The ceremony was impressive. Everyone was dressed in real civilian clothes sent from home. Even the two infantry squads protecting the chapel didn't detract from the moment. A couple of friends from Patti's unit sang "Bridge over Troubled Waters."

After our vows were spoken, we went outside to a helicopter that had "Just Married" written on it and smoke grenades on the skids. Trailing red, green, and white smoke, we took off toward the 85th and the reception. I couldn't help thinking, "She is right. Even if it's only for a day, it will be a day in which we are truly one."

The reception was a party that would have made any real trooper, past or present, proud. It overflowed with loud music, dancing, and general craziness. They all wanted this celebration to be as much theirs as Patti's and mine. We wanted them to feel that way. Our friends had been a part of what brought Patti and me together.

About the time things were getting somewhat rowdy and the sound level was killing fish in the pond outside, Patti told me she was going to our "suite" and for me to come over soon. Half an hour later I snuck out a back door.

Looking for the nursing supervisor I'd encountered before, I ran over to Patti's(our) room. I opened the door and there she stood.

She was a sight to behold, dressed in sheer white silk. She was all I could ever want. One odd thing though: she was cooking bacon.

"Excuse me, dear," I said, "but are you always going to greet me after a hard day's work dressed like that and cooking? If so, you'd better get used to cold meals."

"Some of the girls found some fresh eggs and real bacon for our wedding dinner," she explained. "The bacon is only a little off, but I thought we should have it now. If we wait until the next time we get around to it, we'll have to throw it out."

She had just taken the bacon out of the pan to put onto a plate when the scream of air raid sirens interrupted us.

I don't know if I heard the rocket coming or felt it in another sense.

I threw Patti on the floor just as an explosion sent hot shrapnel through the roof. Not now, I prayed, please not now!

I grabbed my rifle, gave Patti my pistol and took her to the underground bunker. She in her nightie, me in my suit.

Knowing that in this war rocket attacks usually preceded enemy intruders or "sappers," I went to a bunker near the barbed wire so that I could help watch the perimeter.

Six hours later the all-clear sounded. I went back to our place and there she was. Sound asleep in bed.

She woke up as the door shut behind me. "Hi, honey!" she asked, "Tough day at the office?"

In the same light vein I replied, "You bet, and I'm starved. Where's that bacon?"

Then she explained about our wedding dinner. She had grabbed the plate of bacon as I was pushing her out of the door to the bunker. When she got to the bunker, the fragrance of almost fresh bacon was so appealing to the other nurses that she gave them all an equal share. The concussion from the exploding rocket had knocked the eggs to the floor. They were in the trash.

This day was not going well at all!

Later that afternoon Patti and I were packed and ready to leave on our honeymoon. We had decided to go to Hong Kong for a few days, then back to the States. We both thought it would be a great idea to spend some time with each of our families. Mine lived in Yakima, Washington, and hers in Euclid, Ohio.

We met Steve in the mess hall. He was going to fly us to Da Nang in a scout ship where we would meet an airliner for the trip to Hong Kong.

We said our goodbyes to everyone and soon were on our way. Our flight path took us over a high point in the road between Phu Bai and Da Nang called the Hai Bong Pass.

As we were cruising high over the pass, Steve anxiously pointed down. The enemy was attacking a train. Several passenger cars were burning and even from our altitude we could see civilians being shot as they tried to escape.

Steve sent out an urgent radio message informing operations about the situation. There was little else that we could do. Besides having Patti on board, our ship was unarmed.

We continued toward Da Nang. Steve dropped us off at the air base. He left quickly, claiming that he wanted to get back to the unit and get some rest after all the wedding festivities.

Only after our return to the base weeks later did we hear that he had gone back to the burning train. He had flown low and fast between the enemy machine-gunners and tried to draw fire away from the civilians. His aircraft had been hit and he had been wounded slightly in both legs. He had crashed but by some miracle had managed to be rescued. Steve spent two weeks in the hospital before returning to our unit.

Our flight to Hong Kong was scheduled for the next morning. We spent the night in Da Nang. Unfortunately, the base had no joint quarters available. There was no reason to have them. Who would have expected a married couple here? Patti was assigned to the women's barracks and I to the men's. I decided this war was becoming more than a little inconvenient.

The next morning we were on our way to Hong Kong and the Empress Hotel. A grand place to stay; it even had hot and cold running water *inside* . . . a real novelty for us.

We shopped for wedding rings. A simple gold band for me and a gold band and a diamond for Patti. We also bought clothes. Lots and lots of clothes and not one item army green.

On our last night in Hong Kong we ate at the Floating Restaurant where our a seven-course meal was courtesy of our very pleased tailor. All in all, we had a wonderful time.

We left Hong Kong behind, heading for the United States and home. As we flew over Washington state, Patti was amazed at how beautifully clear and green it was around Seattle. It was one of those rare days when the sun was shining and the view of lush forests and snowcapped mountains was endless. It seemed to be a day saved up especially to impress my new wife. I was born in the Seattle area and have never seen such a spectacular day before or since.

We went to our farm in Yakima and Patti was welcomed with open arms. When I could corner Mom alone, I was finally able to explain why I had been so cranky on my last visit home. I had been missing Patti. Even home was no-place without her.

That evening I took Patti to our peach orchard where I had first decided to make her my wife. This time we watched the sunset together.

I awoke early the next morning and went downstairs where I discovered, not to my surprise, that my mother was in the kitchen. The house, except for her soft foot-steps, was quiet.

Not knowing I was there, I watched her. The smell of fresh coffee was strong. It was a large kitchen. She moved within it, knowingly. The pleasure of having family near and the love she felt for everyone was on her face.

For a moment we were alone. Just she and I. Together but at the same time, worlds apart.

If I had never realized her wisdom, patience, and un-derstanding before, I was soon to learn. Sensing my pres-ence, she turned toward me. From her apron she pulled a letter and handed it to me.   Recognizing my own words I glanced at the pages, then her.

I had written the letter several months earlier when I was home on leave. I had only roughed it out and later left it in my bedroom desk drawer. I don't believe I really meant it to be read. In a way, I think it was just a reaffirmation to myself that what I was doing in Vietnam was acceptable in my own mind. Maybe I was confused about how others looked at what I was doing and because I cared how they felt about me, I wanted to give them an explanation. Maybe it was a look into my future. Maybe a goodbye. Maybe—?

In its entirety, this is the letter she gave me:

Dearest Family,

I want you all to know how much I love you. I am sorry if I have caused you any undue concern or worry by my returning to Vietnam. I have found that, looking within myself, it is something I must do.

I have traveled the world since I was very young. I have seen hunger, pain, and dissent in Hong Kong, Thailand, India, and now Vietnam. As sad as it may be to say, I have also had these same experiences in America.

I have always been willing to fight, both by giving of my mind and body, to help those who have less than I and needed me. I am only one of many thousands who share these same emotions and desires.

Now, as a member of our Armed Forces, I believe the people of Vietnam require a gift. A gift of my protection.

I realize this seems a weak and unstable rationale to some of my friends, but, to me, it is a reason of passion.

During my first tour of duty in Vietnam, although we have rarely spoken of it, one of my missions was to help innocent citizens be fed, clothed, and protected against an unrelenting enemy. I tried hard to see that this was accomplished.

However, as a helicopter pilot, I am also committed to fighting a war. Right or wrong, these are also my duties. I must support my fellow troopers in the field. As you so well know, on my last mission I was wounded several times and my aircraft shot down attempting to rescue several of our injured and unarmed soldiers.

Still I am willing to return. I know full well the hazards I face and the pain my doing so may inflict upon you and those who love me.

If my one life, as dear as it is to me, can help save the life of just one other, then it is my life I must risk.

I have recently met another who shares the same dreams, desires, and hope for the future in which you and I believe. She is a special person in my life. She understands the risks I take and why. I truly love her. I can only pray that you may someday meet her.

I know you worry about me. Please try to understand those things we may never truly understand.

I will always love you.

Love,
John

The words I had written on the paper my mother had handed me stared back at me.

Mom, unblinking, spoke, "John," she said, "I love you but I don't believe in this so-called war. You don't have the perspective we at home do. The protests and sit-ins. In my mind too many are dying for the wrong reasons.

"I read your letter. It gave me a chance to look into your heart and I have never faulted you for following your heart. You truly believe in what you're doing. Do all you believe you must."

"You love Patti and without question she loves you. Although I can't believe in the war, I *can* believe that a few people like you and Patti can bring back the lessons you've learned together and make a difference here at home for the future. Take advantage of your experiences and most of all, the soul-binding love you and Patti have for each other. We need you both here. When the time is right, the opportunity will make itself available."

She continued, "I love Patti also. Please—a mother's promise—we'll never mention this again. The only thing that matters is that you both come home safe and, most of all, together."

"Yes, mother," I answered, surprised at her words.

"The sun is coming up. I know you and Patti fulfilled a dream to walk in the orchard. Fulfill one for me before you leave. Let's see a new day rise together," she asked.

We did.

Days later, Patti and I flew to Ohio. Patti's parents met us at the airport and drove us to their home, where I was introduced to the rest of her family.

The entire neighborhood had hung a huge sign with "Welcome Home Patti and John" printed in red, white, and blue. They were having a block party in our honor.

I shared war stories with veterans of World War II and Korea and explained to curious children what the ribbons I wore on my uniform represented. Meeting friends, eating pizza, and sleeping late were wonderful luxuries.

Before long the time arrived to go back to Vietnam. Although leaving was difficult, both of us had a duty to fulfill. Again, in what seemed only a few short hours, we were back in the middle of a war.

I arrived at my unit and met my new CO. Fortunately he was kind enough to let me continue using the helicopter to fly to Patti each night. As long as I was back for the first mission the next day and the ship was properly maintained, he had no quarrels.

It was business as usual.

✦ ✦ ✦

One must remember that, even though being a scout pilot held some occasionally dangerous moments and fast times, much more time was spent waiting than actually on missions.

At first light in the morning, our entire platoon would report to the flight line. This meant all fit pilots, gunners and mechanics, officers and enlisted, would be available. The only exclusions were those who were ill or had been on guard duty the night before. The aircraft were pre-flighted, checked again, armed, fueled, personal gear and weapons stored, and flight readiness reports filed.

When the first mission was launched for the morning recon, no one had much to do until the next relief mission departed, usually in about an hour. Some guys had other duties during that time. There were the full barrels from the "outhouse" latrines to be collected and burned. And sand bags to be filled. I doubt there is a grain of Vietnamese soil that hasn't been shoveled into a bag somewhere along the line. A lot of guys just went back to bed. A few just hung around the flight line and hoped something would happen.

My gunner, Bill, became the epitome of the word "happening."

For some unknown reason, one day he wondered to himself if, by loosening the cartridge from a pistol shell casing and igniting the exposed powder with a match, would the bullet just "pop" into the air?

"It isn't even dangerous. Couldn't hurt a thing," he said.

Having an unlimited amount of ammunition, Bill began to experiment. Before long he had graduated from the 38 caliber pistol rounds to 5.53 mm rounds, 7.62 rounds then, finally, 50 caliber bullets. They are very large. He favored 50 caliber tracer projectiles because as they shot straight up, at about thirty-five feet of altitude, the phosphorous would ignite and produce a short light show.

Bill became a real side attraction for awhile. Mr. Entertainment.

I finally closed the curtain when I saw him prying apart a 40 mm grenade, "Just to see how it works, sir."

Shortly after I told Bill no more performances, he invented what he termed his new "secret weapon." He called it a "zeke bomb." I decided not to ask how he arrived at this title.

I had been stuck with some extra missions about the time Bill was perfecting his new toy. Because of the additional flight time, I had not been able to see Patti for three or four days. My attitude was, shall we say, far from perky.

I was sitting on the steps in front of our hootch trying to get interested in a book. Bill walked up carrying an ammo can. It looked heavy.

"What I have here, LT, is the end to this war as we know it," he said. "Unless," I answered, "you have a pocket full of blank honorable discharges in your pocket, don't bring up the subject."

Gently, he sat the can down . . . very gently. "Look here," he said. He opened the top slowly. Inside, stuffed together, I saw fragmentation grenades, white phosphorous grenades, plastic explosives, nails, glass, and something that looked like, maybe, water buffalo dung. (Not that I'm an expert on water buffalo dung).

"It's great for dropping down enemy tunnels," he stated. I could only think that if it managed to go off, hopefully outside the aircraft, it most certainly would make enough noise to at least confuse any enemy.

Bill's pleasure in what he had produced and my curiosity in this weird grouping of killing devices, took me away from my book.

It wasn't long before he convinced me to take his creation along on our next mission. When I said, "Yes, OK," Bill grinned like the Cheshire Cat.

In a heartbeat Bill was headed to the flight line and stowing his new toy aboard our ship.

It wasn't long before I heard the ominous ring of our platoon's mission call telephone. Telephone is a poor description. You spoke in a strange horn shaped device, held another separate device to your ear, and either screamed to be heard or were screamed at to be heard. A hand crank operated the "ringer." Strictly World War I. Vietnam was not always the high-tech war it has been made out to be.

Being the next pilot up for a mission, I answered the phone. I was informed that one of our infantry platoons was engaged in a firefight with a unit of North Vietnamese not far to our west.

I ran to my ship and started the engine. Bill jumped aboard as I increased power and we prepared for takeoff. I turned around to Bill; he gave me a "thumbs up."

But, for some reason, when I tried to pick the aircraft up to a hover and move it out of its protective barriers, it would not fly.

I checked my instruments. Everything was normal. My power reading said I should fly. The ship just would not lift.

I turned to Bill again and told him the only thing I could think of as the problem was we might be overloaded. We had to hurry, jettison what we didn't really need and take off or the Cobras, who had already departed, would leave us behind. We had to get going. "Now, thank you very much!"

It seems Bill had put five of his new "bombs" aboard. Each one must have weighed a hundred pounds. With great anguish, he carefully off-loaded four of the canisters. I stared at him, frowning, now that I realized what our weight problem was. He glanced around, looking from me to his last bomb and back again. "OK," I said "but only one. Let's go." We bounced down the tarmac, got airborne and struggled to catch up with the Cobras. We were still a little heavy. About a hundred pounds or so.

When we arrived over the ground unit engaged with the enemy, we were immediately briefed on the situation. I went down on the trees forward of our troops' position to begin my recon and if possible, draw fire away from our ground people.

The enemy, realizing they were now out-gunned, began to withdraw. On one of our low-level passes, Bill saw several small groups of enemy jumping into "spider holes." These were well-hidden entrances to tunnels and hiding areas underground. They did more than just protect them from possible air strikes. In some cases, if our troops were in pursuit, the enemy could hide, wait, and then jump out to attack from the rear.

There was little we could do to flush them out with our machine guns. They were also too small a target to be hit accurately with the rockets from the Cobras. I could only inform the infantry of their positions.

Moments later we were asked to give support to another platoon about a half a mile away that had just made contact with the enemy.

On arrival, the ground commander pointed out that he was receiving heavy weapons fire along a tree line across a clearing from their position. Two of his men were wounded and in the clearing.

Could we, he asked, do something to keep the enemy's heads down so some of his people could move forward and bring back his wounded?

"No problem," I answered.

I began making gun runs on the opposite tree line. The Cobras, flying even lower than usual, were close behind and firing at the muzzle flashes from the enemy weapons as they shot at me.

Again, nothing was more important to us than an American life. In situations like this when we could definitely make the difference between one of our own living or dying, we all hung our necks out a little more than usual.

Finally the two wounded were rescued and brought back to our own lines. The enemy, at least those that were able, withdrew into the jungle.

Unfortunately, the two rescues had taken a little longer than expected. Bill and I were both out of ammunition. The Cobras were also expended.

Naturally, the platoon that we had gone to support earlier now radioed that their point men were pinned down by a couple of enemy soldiers who were next to a spider hole. Could we assist? Murphy's Law.

The lead Cobra pilot was explaining that we were out of ammo; they'd have to wait for another team. We would, though, stay until they arrived. In the meantime, we'd act as a radio relay and briefing station between them and main base.

Hearing this, Bill said over the intercom, "Say, LT, I've still got my 'zeke bomb'."

"Do you think that thing will work?" I asked.

"Guaranteed," he answered.

"It better," I said.

I called the Cobras and explained our plan.

The enemy didn't know we were out of ammo. If indeed it was just a couple of guys next to a spider hole that had our troopers pinned down, chances were they'd go back down the hole when they heard us coming. Besides, we had a "secret weapon" aboard.

"A what?" said Cobra lead. "Never mind. It sounds good. It's your show. Sic 'em, boy."

Sure enough, as we approached the enemy position, down the hole they went. The point men who had been under fire guided us directly over the tunnel entrance.

Bill was beautiful to watch. As we hovered over the hole, he ignited the fuse on his bomb and pushed the heavy canister out the door. He looked as proud as a father sending his firstborn off to college. Down the hole it went.

"I suggest we get out of here, lieutenant," Bill said.

As we moved away, the explosions started. First a couple small ones, then a few larger, and then one huge blast! You could have driven a truck into the crater that was left.

The infantry platoon leader radioed me. "I'm impressed, little bird. Thanks. As soon as my ears clear, we'll be moving out. I owe you one."

"We aim to please," I said.

On the way back to base, I told Bill that I, too, was impressed.

From then on, whenever Bill and I flew together, our ship was always a little heavier than usual.

About a hundred pounds or so.

As I've mentioned, many of our missions required us to fly very low and very slow. Usually too slow and low for my comfort. Bill, being the maniac he was, ate it up. The lower and slower the better.

Unlike me, one of Bill's favorite situations was the morning perimeter recon mission. It met all his prerequisites for what he termed a "hot date."

Every third or fourth day each scout had to take a "tour" around our main base just before sunup. This was to make sure enemy sappers had not infiltrated our perimeter during the night. It was a normal mission, rarely exciting and usually accomplished with just one scout ship flying without cover aircraft.

The mission was a real pain. If there had been enemy activity the night before, the sentry personnel, assuming they were awake, would have spotted them. Patrols were out patrolling. Other guards had infrared night goggles. There were also "tripwires" laid out on the ground and various other heights. These wires, if touched by someone trying to crawl over, under, or through would set off lord only knows how many alarms.

As a rather lazy pilot who knew "first light" missions required having to be pre-flighted, armed, and in the air before breakfast mess—let alone coffee—was served, I didn't look forward to these mornings. Like it or not, I took my turn. If memory serves me, I drew this particular mission with a low card after a late night poker game.

This mission, unfortunately, trailed on the heels of Bill's now infamous "zeke bomb" trick. Bill was, of course, my gunner that morning.

Consider being tired and cranky, then add sharing a confined space with a hyperactive, nineteen-year-old crazy person at 4:30 A.M., who now believed that every post hole dug in the area in the last one-hundred years was a spider hole concealing crack NVA troops. It's exactly what everyone needs to start a day.

Just before climbing aboard for takeoff, Bill had been hopping around like a puppy on hot asphalt. "Hey, lieutenant," he said, "can you believe we got this job. Great, huh!" I wanted to slap him. I still couldn't believe the low card was a jack of clubs. I'd have to check that deck.

On departure I called control and told them we were up and operating. No answer. Probably in bed, I thought.

All I could think of was breakfast. Let's get this over with. Bill, on the other hand, was chatting up a storm. I'd seen him like this before. It should have been a warning: "Bill wants to shoot something. Let him get it out of his system and let's go home." I didn't listen to myself.

It was my intention to set a new speed record for flying around our base perimeter. About five minutes into the recon Bill yelled into the microphone, "LT, spider hole!" I almost jumped out of my seat from my semi-sleep.

I was looking out the starboard side of the aircraft when he yelled. I assumed we were both seeing the same very old and very large bomb crater.

Before I could catch my breath to tell Bill to "put a sock in it," I noticed a grenade—minus the pin—departing Bill's hand overboard ever so slowly.

Normally this would not have been a problem.

This was not a normal problem.

As it so happened, at the same time Bill had caught me off guard by screaming about the alleged spider hole, I, seeing only a bomb crater, flared the aircraft to a hover to show him otherwise. When he had let the grenade go out the door he naturally figured it would fly out behind the helicopter due to our forward airspeed.

It didn't. We didn't have any forward airspeed.

Out the door it went and landed directly on our right helicopter skid.

There it sat.

I swear I have never looked at anything so hard for what seemed so long in my entire life. All Bill could say was, "Oh-oh." For those not in the know, those little devils have a rather short fuse.

I immediately threw the control cyclic hard left to clear our aircraft from what I knew would soon be a noisy explosion very near a still quiet main base.

Of course the grenade, having been handcrafted and built in America, did just at it was designed to do—it went bang.

It was now 4:40 a.m.

Everything sort of went downhill from there.

Hearing the explosion, every machine gunner on that side of the bunker line let loose. This in itself wasn't bad. Unfortunately I was doing what I did best, flying low and slow. I was also down range from the return fire from about one-hundred of our own now very wide-awake security troops.

To make matters worse, if that was possible, I began yelling at Bill over the intercom. He couldn't hear me over the blast of his M-60 machine gun. He had opened fire thinking that if one-hundred other people were shooting, maybe there was even more enemy out there. The noise was deafening and we were on the wrong end of most of it.

In my panic to scream at Bill, it turned out I wasn't pressing my intercom button. I was transmitting.

Well, it seems that some intellectual jerk back in the Pentagon some years before had decided that trip flares should also have the capability of being set off by certain radio frequencies. I was on that frequency.

My informing Bill on my transmitting radio that I was going to choke him, assuming we ever made it to the ground in one piece, was merrily setting off every flare in our immediate vicinity.

The more I hollered at Bill over the radio the better the light show.

Camp Eagle, our main base, was a rather large place. Had I had a choice, all this would have happened either to some other poor pilot or, at the very least, the southwest corner of base where there were the fewest gentlemen of, should we say, higher authority.

No way.

It happened within 400 yards of the personal hootch of none other than *the* man himself—the commanding general of the entire 101st Airborne Division.

He wasn't known to be a pleasant individual when dealing with lieutenants on the best of days. Especially in the early morning.

It was 4:45 A.M.

The general was now awake. He was not amused and if he couldn't get answers to "just what is going on," he wanted "somebody's head."

There is little doubt that a lieutenant's head, namely mine, with or without a silver platter, would have brightened his day.

There were a lot of people at that early hour trying to save theirs. It didn't take them long to find me.

When we finally landed, the MPs were waiting. Bill, not waiting for the aircraft to shut down, departed the scene. The last words I heard him utter were, "See ya."

Gone. No Bill.

I was escorted from the flight line to the general's hootch with much pomp and circumstance. The red lights on the MP jeeps were flashing everywhere in the early morning.

Before I left the flight line with the MPs, Bill had time to make it to the scout hootch and wake up anyone who wasn't already awake. He let them know I was being hauled away for some possible act of treason.

As we drove through our compound my friends gave me lots of support.

"Remember, name, rank, and serial number only, John!" yelled one.

"Patti's mine," said another as we passed by.

Most of the rest of what I heard was mere laughter and hooting.

I was told that Weird Bob, standing at the scout hootch stairs wearing absolutely nothing, had turned to Mike and asked, "Do you think there'll be a firing squad? I'd like that. I've never seen one before. By the way, why is everyone up so early?"

The MP captain sitting next to me asked, "Those your friends?" "Yes," I replied. "Get others," he said.

I knew these guys. They were probably already plotting a way to break me out.

Actually, I learned later they had all gone back to bed.

At 6:15 A.M., after a very long wait, I stood before our general.

Just he and I were in his office. I watched his mouth move and the veins in his neck get bigger.

I couldn't exactly hear everything he was yelling about. My ears were still ringing a little from the "combat" I had been in earlier.

Soon I noticed, though, that he wasn't yelling quite so much anymore. He stopped talking and sort of stared at me.

"Say, don't I know you?" he asked. "Oh yes, that's right. You're one of those fine representatives of our officer corps who stole my bell!"

"You're Lieutenant Hendrix," he whispered.

He remembered my name.

About a month before, several other scouts and I were caught stealing a big brass bell engraved with the general's name from the Command Officers Club. Unfortunately, that particular bell seemed to have a special place in the general's heart. It looked like any other brass bell with a leather handle attached to the clapper. We even had one at home on our front door, only smaller.

There was a difference. The bell we "borrowed" wasn't the one from my front door. I wish it had been.

This special brass engraved bell had been presented to the general when he was a young officer in Korea—as a lieutenant, I'd heard. A rank he'd most likely forgotten he'd ever held. It had been given to him by his platoon. To him the bell was important.

The bell hung in the general's personal mess and staff club where people like the other scouts and I were not welcome unless invited.

I'm still not sure what set us all off.

There we were, sitting around our own little ramshackle officers club built from whatever spare rocket boxes we could find: Steve, me, Weird Bob, Mike, Jim—basically every scout in the platoon plus a couple of Snake drivers and three or four Huey pilots. Everyone was just hanging out and listening to the music from Woodstock Live. The weather had been nasty and there wasn't much else to do. Jimi Hendrix was my favorite. Besides the fact that we were both from Seattle, I liked his name.

The night wore on.

Later, when the music stopped, Weird Bob made mention of how he had been counting the number of Distinguished Flying Crosses that had been awarded to the members of the unit present that night. "You know," he said, "I'll bet we've set some sort of record. Does anybody else fight this war except us?"

Mike chimed in, "Not only that. Consider the number of missions we've flown, not counting the type of mission." It wasn't unusual to hear this kind of talk. We all believed we were the best. However, the tone of voice that night seemed a little more stressed that normal.

Weird Bob wasn't much of a talker. It was because he had something to say that we all began to listen intently.

One thing used to drive me crazy about Weird Bob. When he did speak, every sentence began with, "You know." He was from California.

"You know," Weird Bob continued, "every time one of us qualifies for an award of some kind for trying to win this war, the general does everything short of mailing it to us. You know, I can't think of even once when any of us have been given something by him personally. You know, it's just 'Here, thanks, bye.'"

Other than saying "Taking fire" or "Rolling in" I don't think I'd ever heard Weird Bob put so many words together in any one twenty-four hour period.

In any case, many of the pilots present that night, having had more than several drinks, agreed with Weird Bob.

I was one of them.

The trouble started in earnest when Jim spoke up. "That's not really true. When I got my Silver Star, the general invited me over to the command staff bar for a drink. He personally rang that bell of his that's behind his bar and announced me to the crowd."

"No," said Steve. "I heard the real story. The only reason the general did that was because some *Stars and Stripes* newspaper bigwig was around. The general wanted to look like a people-sort-of guy. I've heard it before. It's the old I-love-the-troops-and-the-troops-love-me thing. He wanted an opportunity to ring that bell of his and tell a reporter, 'Yes, this is so-and-so. He did something today. Whatever it was. But I know you're really wondering why I rang this beautiful brass bell with my name engraved on it. It's an example of how my men feel about me.' . . . Did you ever see the story that was published that was suppose to be about you?" asked Steve.

"Sure I did," said Jim. "I even sent it to my Dad. Wait! Yeah, you're right. My name wasn't in the story. Maybe the bell did get first billing. Still, my Dad said he liked the blurb after I filled in the blank spots that were left out. Like my name, my medal," he said as an afterthought.

"I've heard he rings the bell if someone walks in and doesn't have shined boots," a Huey pilot said. We all looked around. Most of us were wearing shower clogs. "And then," he continued, "you have to buy everyone in the bar a drink. Those boys don't drink the cheap stuff, brother."

Again everyone slowly looked around. There had been a long-standing rumor that anything ordered at our club had been cut down with a little jet fuel.

A Snake pilot with rather glassy eyes spoke up, "Some-one told me that if he doesn't like your looks he'll ring the bell and, with everyone else staring at you, he makes you clean his latrine with a toothbrush. Just like flight school."

"I'll bet he laughs while doing it," said someone.

In my head I could hear Bill's infamous words, "Oh-oh." Unfortunately I had had too much jet fuel to remember the rest of what Bill had said, "Lieutenant, let's get out of here."

As fate would have it, I sat there nodding in agreement. At the time it seemed more fun being here than walking back to my hootch in the rain. Patti was working a split shift and, with the weather the way it was, I wouldn't see her for a few days. So, I stayed.

The conversation grew more heated. Of course, at the same time, more drinks were being ordered and consumed.

After a while, Weird Bob broke in, "You know, that bell of the general's is an example of what's wrong with this war. No respect for the little guy. We should do something about it!"

"Like what?" asked Jim.

Steve spoke next, "Let's go over there and tell the general we don't like his bell!"

There we were. Fifteen "ace" pilots, hammered to the gills, with nothing better to do than go tell the commanding general of the US Army's most crack airborne unit we didn't like his brass bell.

It made sense at the time.

It sure didn't later.

Before we even started, we had a problem. In our unit, officers weren't allowed to drive. We pilots could fly very expensive aircraft but not drive a $2,000 jeep.

It was too far to walk in the mud. How would we get to the general's club?

The problem was solved when some industrious soul, while relieving himself out the front door of our club, noticed an unoccupied jeep.

The keys were in it.

For a bunch of guys who spent their days destroying enemy equipment, borrowing one of our own jeeps for a little while seemed a minor offense.

After all, weren't we taxpayers? It was partly ours.

The next question was, who would drive? This was a more serious problem. Only duly trained and licensed personnel were allowed to operate an army vehicle. None of us qualified. Not one of us had a license. Without much hesitation, Jim had an idea. "Forget the license. I've got some sergeant rank pins in my pocket. One of my troops is getting promoted tomorrow. I was going to give them to him. If someone would consider taking his bars off, put these on, then, if we do get pulled over—hey—a sergeant is driving. The MPs will just figure he's got a license. Besides, who's going to argue with this many officers?"

I was lucky. My bars were sewn on. Steve, on the other hand, wore pin-on bars. Easy on, easy off.

"I'm your man," Steve said. "Put them on me. Do me a favor. Make sure they're on straight. I do have some pride."

Off we went, the pride of the Air Cavalry. One jeep, one driver who couldn't find second gear if his life depended on it, and fourteen others in, on, or hanging from a vehicle built for, at the most, five people.

Believe it or not we did get pulled over by the MPs. We were only about one-hundred yards from the general's staff club.

The MPs were actually very polite at first, considering. They explained that the beer bottles being thrown by "various individuals from said vehicle" had sort of gotten their attention.

"And where are you going, sirs?" they asked.

"To capture the general's brass bar bell, pig," Weird Bob said.

"Sorry," Steve said, "he's not well." Steve's elbow in Weird Bob's ribs shut him up for a minute.

"Yeah. Sure," the MPs said.

"OK, driver, how about some ID," the MP next to Steve demanded. The MP in charge tried hard to ignore the rest of us.

"I'm sorry, officer, I don't have it on me," Steve explained.

With that answer, hopefully more out of habit than anything, two MPs put their hands on their billy clubs, while the other MP slowly reached toward the flap of his pistol holder.

The MP standing next to Steve in our open jeep said, "Do I have to tell you this is a war zone? You can be shot for not having proper ID on this base, especially being this close to HQ."

So much for military secrets.

Steve took out his ID from his jacket pocket. He cautiously passed it to the MP next to him.

After the MP read over Steve's ID card he calmly said, "Look, lieutenant, I don't know what's going on here. I don't really care. I get off shift in two hours. You're all having fun. Good! Just stay out of trouble. Now, go home. And please, never let anyone know this ever happened!"

"Thanks," Steve said.

"What, no salute, pig!" yelled Weird Bob. Another elbow.

"Don't push it, sir," snapped the MP.

The MPs drove away.

Did we turn around? Nope. Straight to the general's mess we went.

Moments later we arrived. We immediately had another problem.

We had never decided who were to be the "volunteers" to actually steal the bell. The supply of beer we had started with was fast running low, as was our courage. While we were all arguing, someone noticed that Jim and Weird Bob were missing.

Before anyone could say, "Where'd they go?" here they came. At a dead run.

As they ran all we heard was, "Let's get out of here!" Clang, clang. "Hurry up!" Clang, clang. "Start the jeep—drive!" Clang, clang.

I have no idea to this day who was driving. Behind us I heard angry shouting voices. I swear there were pistol shots.

We actually made it all the way back to our unit before we were met by a platoon of MPs.

A couple of them seemed familiar.

They didn't have to look too hard for us.

Steve's ID, fourteen rather crazed soldiers all wearing officer bars and pilots wings, air cavalry insignia, and, of course, a stolen jeep with our unit's name written on the hood and bumpers sort of gave us away.

Our CO heard the MPs side of the story. Dressed in a silk robe, he walked up to us.

"OK, who's got the bell?" he asked.

"Bell, sir?" someone asked.

"The bell—now."

I knew that tone of voice. I'd heard him use it in the A Shau Valley on a few missions.

This wasn't a game with him anymore.

There was a stirring, then a shuffle of feet.

Moments later a green laundry bag with a muffled clang inside was passed forward.

"Here sir," two or three of us said in unison.

Still frowning, he said, "Thank you." Holding the bag in one hand, the other hand raised high, he walked toward the MPs.

As he gave them the bell, he turned back to us, winked, and, in just one corner of his mouth, smiled. Making the sign of the cross over his chest, he spoke quietly, "May God have mercy on our souls."

A few very long hours later, fifteen junior officers stood before their general.

I was one.

We could only hope that, at best, due to our number, he wouldn't shoot all of us. Maybe just a few as an example.

After all the yelling the general did, I really believed that, had we been in an earlier time and another war, he might have done just that plus more.

We were all at attention in his office. He paraded up and down our little formation memorizing our name tags.

No matter what anyone says about that man, there's one thing nobody can argue about—his ability to remember names was fantastic.

When he finished telling us how we had dishonored him, the airborne, the officer corps, him, the army as a whole, the president, him again, and much, much more, I was too hung over to care or remember what had been said. We were marched off by our CO.

As much as the general probably wanted us shot, he managed to decide upon a worse punishment. When we weren't flying missions we were to spend all our waking hours filling sandbags. For a week.

Getting shot down and taken prisoner started to look like a step up.

Sandbags were filled. The MPs who had stopped us that night and let us go were ordered to monitor us. They made sure there were no mistakes. Actually, they made sure we moved dirt up to the hour, minute, and second of our assigned week.

In war there is no mercy.

✦　✦　✦

Now, another week or so later, after waking up the entire base, I stood again before my general.

As I said, he had a great knack for remembering names. He certainly seemed to remember mine.

"Aren't you one of my junior officers who was involved in that bell incident? Yes, that's right. Lieutenant Hendrix, correct?"

I tried to stand straight. I could only hope for mercy. I still dreamt of those sand bags.

"Yes, sir!" I said.

Then, he smiled. He almost laughed.

He sat down behind his desk and motioned me to sit in a nearby metal frame chair.

I felt like a condemned man. Make the other guy sit down and relax, then throw the switch.

The general leaned back, turned toward the ceiling, and started talking. He wasn't necessarily talking to me because I was there but, in a way, he seemed to be talking for the sake of it.

He told me about some of the stunts he'd pulled at West Point. He even mentioned a few crazy things he'd been a part of as a young officer. Some of his pranks made our bell joke look pretty tame.

He seemed to forget that I was there because, with Bill's assistance, I had been responsible for engaging the entire 101st Airborne with nonexistent enemy troops.

The more he chatted the more I realized what was happening. I'd seen it before, but never from a person with a star on his uniform. He was tired. Just like the rest of us, he was tired.

After a few minutes he caught himself and sat up. "Let's get some breakfast," he suggested. Over oven-fried bacon and real eggs in his personal mess area, the general and I were served our meal by a young Vietnamese girl. She was about twenty years old. When she spoke to the general I noticed her English was excellent.

As we ate, he explained how he truly believed in what we were doing to support the Vietnamese people.

I agreed with the general but, as an infantry officer, I said I had a little problem with fight, pull back, fight, stand by, wait policies.

Our almost father-and-son conversation ended immediately. Suddenly his eyes flashed at me.

"Just do as you're told. It's your duty. I have work to do. Good day, lieutenant."

I stood and saluted as he left. Before I could sit back down, my plate and coffee cup disappeared from the table.

Breakfast was over.

I did manage to grab a hard roll on the way out. It was for Bill. I was reasoning that bread and water for a day or two for him might even things out a bit.

During the following two weeks, on two different occasions and after completing normal recon missions, I heard over the radio, "Well done."

It sounded like our general's voice.

I don't doubt he told everyone "well done" if he was in that area and monitoring his radio from his command and control helicopter. It's just that those two times, believing it was him, were special to me.

Another week passed. Bill and I had been assigned another morning "first light" mission as a part of our normal rotation.

Just minutes after takeoff, Bill spotted three enemy troops crawling under the barbed wire on our perimeter. I also saw them. I requested permission to open fire. This time I was on a radio frequency that wouldn't set off all the trip flares that had made me so well known in the past.

After a short delay, permission was granted. We immediately engaged the enemy, killing all three where they lay in the wire.

Later that morning, Special Forces troopers retrieved the bodies. All three were well armed and, without question, saboteurs.

Two were men. The third was a now forever young, no longer pretty Vietnamese girl. It was the girl who had served the general and me our breakfast not long before.

I never heard from or spoke to the general again while I was in Vietnam.

Maybe it was coincidental. Maybe it was on purpose.

Whatever the reason, I missed those occasional radio calls: "Well done."

# Chapter 8

A gain, I don't want to make it sound like all our missions were into the "jaws of death." Much of what we did was little more than takeoff, look around, and return to base. However, sometimes it was the jobs that were supposed to be routine and tame that became the most difficult. These are the missions no one ever forgets.

Bill, our cover team, and I were ordered to do a recon of the ocean coastline just east of main base. We had been in that area several times before. Bill and I enjoyed seeing the beaches and smelling the salt air. It was another of those small things that reminded us of home.

It was also the first and only mission that ever caused a personal problem between Bill and me.

We attended our mission briefing session. We were told that there was little enemy activity where we were headed. This job was merely the usual show of force.

I decided to depart base flying low rather than going to altitude with the Snakes and then coming back down later. It wasn't far to where we were going. Besides, flying low into an area where the chances of getting shot at were slim was fun.

Actually, flying low was always fun. Not getting shot at made it better.

Shortly after takeoff we reached the beach. It was beautiful. Pure white sand bordered by tall green trees and emerald waters. It was different from our rocky beaches and dark waters in Washington state but close enough.

Bill raised his arm and pointed across the ocean. "Home, James."

"Don't tempt me," I answered.

Bill and I were playing, weaving in and out of the trees then flying just inches from the beach when the lead Cobra radioed us.

"Sorry to interrupt your vacation, 14. We enjoyed watching you play," he said. I didn't like his tone of voice.

"Something's come up to our west," he continued. "Nobody's given us the mission but I think we should reposition just in case we're needed."

"Roger," I called, "I'm with you."

I was sure Bill had heard what was happening but I wanted to confirm it.

"Bill, did you get that message from overhead?"

"Yeah," he said. He didn't sound pleased. He also didn't end his "Yeah" with "LT" like normal.

I asked if he was OK.

"Yeah." Still no "LT."

We had flown together long enough for me to know he was mad. He was enjoying the beach and now we had to leave. He wasn't ready to leave and, by golly, someone would pay with a hissy fit.

I was that someone.

For starters, Bill decided he wouldn't talk to me anymore.

We had learned through experience to listen to our radios, sort out what was important to just us and still maintain some idle chatter inside our ship. Bill was having none of this now. If I said something I even thought was cute, he just stared out his open door. No answer. Oh, well, let him be.

Speaking of radios, we had two. One VHF and one FM. The Cobras had more and those had longer range. They didn't have the same weight restrictions we had due to the differences in aircraft type.

I would have given my eyeteeth to have one of their radios that day just to know where, exactly, we were going. Then again, maybe not. I never liked having to worry any more than necessary.

We flew west.

The A Shau Valley wasn't far away.

Bill still wasn't talking but I could hear him nervously sliding the bolt on his M-60 machine gun back and forth the further west we flew.

The terrain became vaguely familiar.

Bill and I both now knew where we were headed.

We popped over a ridge and there it was; a place I didn't want to revisit.

Ripcord.

It was the first time Bill and I had been back since it was overrun. I could taste a hint of bile in the back of my throat.

My thoughts of impending doom were broken by a call from our Cobra lead ship.

"Here's the deal, 14," he said. "One of our longrange Ranger units took an NVA officer prisoner last night. They're on the edge of a very small LZ. When I told HQ that we were moseying over this way, they decided you should be the one to fly him out. Sorry. Nobody else is around except you that's small enough to get him out of their tiny LZ."

He continued, "The Rangers can't 'pop smoke' to ID the LZ. They don't want to give away their position until they have to. Besides, when you fly in, they're compromised. They're going to have to head out as soon as you're done."

"I have a general location on them," he said, "but they're hard to hear. They can only whisper on the radio because the enemy is so close. I'll direct you as best as I can. You'll have to pick them up visual then get in and get out as fast as possible. They have a long walk to their own pickup zone. Let's not make this any more difficult than necessary. OK?"

I managed nothing more than two slow clicks on my radio button. That's the universal code for, "Sure, OK, but I don't like it."

I turned to Bill. "Ready, big guy?" I asked. No response. At least now he had a reason not to talk. I didn't feel much like talking myself.

I began my search for the Ranger position at the top of the hill where the firebase used to be and zigzagged down slope into the valley.

As a scout, I was trained to search for anything unusual. Yet, here I was, trying to find some of our own troops, all dressed in green, hiding in a green jungle on the edge of a small green LZ that, for all I knew, could be any one of a hundred bomb craters.

They weren't exactly jumping up and down to draw attention to themselves.

Cobra cockpits are usually pretty quiet, at least compared to something like what I was in with no doors, but even they were having a problem hearing the quiet voices of the Rangers directing me.

I was getting nowhere with my search. I was getting extremely frustrated. I knew that whatever enemy troops were in the area would, sooner or later, get fed up with us overflying their positions and open fire. So far, they just sat and watched.

Suddenly Bill screamed into the intercom, "There, LT, there!" He was pointing but all I saw was jungle.

"Where, where?" I yelled.

"Are you blind?" Bill hollered.

Trying to stay calm, lowering my voice, I spoke to Bill, "Look, please, just clock me in." He was seeing something I didn't. I had to mellow him out so he could direct us to our target. This no-shooting situation would not last much longer.

After about thirty seconds of Bill telling me which way to turn, I finally saw our objective.

There, on the edge of a small bomb crater, I saw several heavily camouflaged Rangers. Between two of them sat another figure, smaller and dressed in a uniform that was a slightly different shade of green.

Pretending to overfly their position, I suddenly turned toward them at the last moment and carefully, slowly, maneuvered into the tall trees and the crater. The terrain's slope was extremely steep.

It was impossible to land. I moved forward at a slow hover toward the slope and managed to stick the toes of my skids into the soft dirt. My rotor blades were turning just inches from the side of the hill in front of my helicopter.

Everyone involved now knew that every NVA troop within miles was very interested in just why we were landing. They would be on the way.

Knowing this full well, the Rangers didn't waste time.

Two Rangers standing below my left skid literally threw the smaller person I had seen on approach into the back of my helicopter next to Bill. He landed on top of Bill's crate of fragmation grenades.

Bill, as shocked as I, pulled his pistol and pressed the barrel against the enemy officer's head that now shared his back seat.

As I carefully backed out of our very tight LZ, I had a fleeting second to look out my side doors. Where moments before were several Rangers, now there was only brush and tree branches blowing in our rotor wash.

Silently, I wished them Godspeed. It was followed by a quick one for us.

When we cleared the LZ, I dove into the lower valley and stayed low until we neared the first friendly firebase some twenty miles away. Feeling a little more secure, I performed a cyclic climb to reach altitude quickly, joining the Cobras.

While I was doing my job, Bill was having a little drama of his own in the back seat.

I turned around and looked through the small space between the cockpit and gunners position to see Bill. There he was, almost nose to nose with a NVA lieutenant. Bill had his pistol up against the lieutenant's ear. Neither of them was batting an eye much less breathing on a regular basis. I'm sure Bill was just as scared as the other guy.

The lead Snake called me on the radio and said that HQ was very pleased with the operation results. I told them we were also pleased. They added that we were ordered to take our POW to Camp Evans. Specifically, to the Republic of Korea (ROK) compound for interrogation. They were to "pop" green smoke for us when we radioed our position as two minutes away.

I had worked with ROK soldiers during my first tour in Vietnam when I was assigned with the 82nd Airborne

Division. I had also heard some horror stories about what those guys did to prisoners. The ROK officers I had personally met since, though, were always very polite and very professional. I figured the stories I had heard must be false. They wouldn't do that; they were on our side.

We were still many miles from Camp Evans when I began thinking about my new passenger and how I would hope to be treated if I were captured. And how Patti would hope I would be cared for.

Why I did it, I'm not sure, but I turned around in my seat, looked at my enemy and gave him the biggest smile I could gather. I topped it off by taking my left hand from the aircraft collective control and gave him the international "V" sign for peace.

Slowly, ever so slowly, never letting Bill have any doubt about what he was doing, our passenger raised his right hand and carefully returned my "V" sign. There was the hint of a smile on his face.

I had an instant respect for this gentleman.

Looking down the wrong end of a barrel held by a most-upset Bill, his first helicopter ride, being taken prisoner all in one day, and still he was able to make the most of a bad situation. Could I have been that brave? I doubt it.

Bill, on the other hand, didn't approve of my friendly attitude. Basically he "lost it." He began yelling at me.

"Just what are you doing, John? Have you gone crazy? Have you forgotten Phil? How about we give this guy a first-class ticket up front! Maybe you can teach him to fly! You want to make friends with him? Fine! You come back here! Maybe while you're inviting him to dinner he'll manage to cut both our throats! You—"

I pulled the intercom circuit breaker so I wouldn't have to listen to him any more. Even from Bill there was only so much I could allow.

As I approached Camp Evans I spotted the Republic of Korea compound and their promised green smoke. I reduced my speed for landing and continued inbound to a hover and their helipad.

Five of the largest individuals I had ever seen were waiting for us. They were all Korean military police.

I was still at a semihover, just touching ground, when they grabbed our POW. He was safer with Bill.

They threw him on the ground and kicked him repeatedly. His face was bleeding profusely when one of the MPs grabbed his right arm and pulled it behind him. Even over the noise of the turbine I could hear the crack of the bone.

The MPs picked him up off the ground and began to drag him away. The POW's arm was dangling in the dirt as they began to pull him around the corner of a small nearby building by his shirt collar.

I looked into his face. I saw again that small grin that I had seen not long before. With his left hand he gave me the "V" sign. Then, he was gone.

I never tried to find out what happened to him. I simply pulled pitch, flew back to our main base, and went about my normal business.

Bill never said a word on our way home. I'm not sure he even took time to holster his pistol. He wasn't feeling any better than I.

That night I walked out to the flight line and sat on the revetments that protected my helicopter. I lay down, propped my head up with my flack jacket and began thinking of Patti. I later wondered what "He" was thinking about.

About half an hour later I heard footsteps. Thinking it was a sentry, I sat up. It was Bill. He climbed up next to me and, without a word, pulled out a pint of Tequila and two shot glasses.

I hate Tequila.

Bill hates Tequila.

An hour or so later the only thing on that revetment between us was an empty bottle of Tequila.

"Pals?" Bill asked.

"Always," I answered.

And life went on.

✦  ✦  ✦

Enemy action had increased so I was flying three missions a day. Most of these were in "the valley."

It is not possible to continue exposing an aircraft to enemy fire that often on a daily basis without something catastrophic happening.

On one mission I was flying with a new gunner. Bill was ill. As we came down level with the treetops following our descent from a safe altitude with our cover, a camouflaged top was thrown off an enemy 51 caliber antiaircraft gun. They opened fire. Their tracers looked like glowing basketballs shooting past us. Then, even further in front of us, I saw the top come off another camouflaged gun. We were caught in crossfire!

Suddenly, the entire Plexiglas front window on my ship was gone and I was sprayed with broken pieces of sharp plastic. Both the radio and instrument panel were reduced to a burned mass of wires.

Another burst of gunfire from the enemy and my tail rotor was gone along with part of the main overhead rotor. The helicopter began spinning.

Although I managed to recover from the spin, our luck didn't hold. As we overflew a small clearing, I saw about forty enemy infantry. They had a clear shot and took it, hitting my engine.

Now I was flying what could best be described as a stone. My gunner and I both braced ourselves as we hit the trees.

I didn't know what to expect when I finally opened my eyes. It took me a second to realize I was alive. I reached around the bulkhead between us and pushed my gunner. He moved a little, slowly regaining consciousness. I yelled for him to get out before the ship exploded. The helicopter was lying on its left side. I unbuckled my straps, then climbed up and out, falling on my face. My leg had been broken in the crash.

My gunner said he was all right. Grabbing our machine guns and ammunition plus a grenade, we cleared the ship.

In order to prevent the enemy from making use of the aircraft for its parts, especially the radios, I pulled the pin on the grenade and tossed it into the helicopter. Losing a $200,000 helicopter and breaking my leg were bad enough, but I had also blown up my favorite camera. I had left it behind underneath the pilot's seat.

We ran, or hobbled, downhill to the edge of a clearing to set up our position and wait to be rescued. When I reached for my survival radio to talk to the Cobras, it was gone. My gunner volunteered to backtrack and find it while I covered him from enemy attack.

He was about twenty yards away when I heard, "Choi Hoi!"—North Vietnamese for surrender. Two enemy soldiers stepped out between my gunner and me, pointing their Russian AK-47s at him.

I fired two short bursts killing both the enemy troops when a third enemy that I had not seen stood up and looked at me. We both fired at the same time. I was lucky. He was not.

My gunner and I decided to forget the radio. I opened my ammo bag. Inside I always kept two smoke grenades (just in case).

The Cobras had stopped firing and were making low passes. I decided they were not sure where we were and had stopped firing for fear of hitting us. I also realized that we were going to be in major trouble if we didn't do something quickly.

I pulled the pins on the two smoke grenades and threw the canisters into the clearing. Yellow and red smoke billowed upward.

Minutes later we heard the "whop whop" sound of the rescue ship's rotor blades. The slope was too steep for them to land so we were pulled up and inside by long nylon straps that the crew hung out the open helicopter doors.

As we took off, the enemy reached the clearing's edge and opened up with small-arms fire. Everybody on board the helicopter shot back and, once clear of the open area, the Cobras sent in a barrage of rockets and cannon fire.

The enemy guns were silent. I had cheated death again, a little the worse for wear but alive.

The first week in the hospital wasn't bad. I was in plaster up to my hip and Patti was able to visit after her duties were over. She often took me around the compound in a wheelchair and, if no one had an eye on us, we would sneak over to our room.

Fellow servicemen also visited and kept me up-to-date on the missions, their successes, and failures. The two pilots from my rescue ship told me they had counted twenty-six bullet holes in their helicopter when they returned to main base after pulling me out of the jungle. I later gave the bartender at the Officers Club fifty dollars. I couldn't have those two gentlemen buying their own drinks for awhile. They were on me! At twenty-five cents a drink, fifty dollars would last awhile.

Trouble really started during the second week of my hospitalization. Doctors hovered over me a little more often. At first they didn't say much. Just looked at my leg, grunted, and went away.

Then came the message. "We have to talk, John," they said. "The wounds you received on your first tour of duty are affecting the circulation in your leg with this new injury. You may lose your leg without more advanced treatment than we can do here." During my first assignment to Vietnam I had been shot in both legs and had taken a minor wound to my arm. My right ankle had been hit and the bones shattered. Now there was little feeling in my foot.

After the doctors left, Patti came in and told me that she had known for several days that I was going to be sent back to the States to a primary hospital. Her CO had made arrangements for us to go home together. We were leaving the next day. She was to have at least a temporary assignment at the Army hospital near Fort Lewis, Washington, where I was to receive treatment.

We were going home. It was over.

That afternoon I sold my newly stocked collection of captured war souvenirs to an enterprising young pilot and gave the money to Patti for the nuns at the orphanage. I had everything I could ever want. I had Patti and we were going home.

But this was not to be. As I was being loaded onto an Air Force transport ship I heard, "Hi, Army." It was my old pilot friend who had flown me from Saigon when I needed to get to Patti months earlier. We talked awhile until Patti walked up, bags in hand. I introduced them and explained to Patti how he had flown me to Phu Bai when I had decided to ask her to be my wife. Now he had to leave for another flight.

Suddenly Patti's nursing supervisor, the infamous lieutenant colonel, was standing there with us. "I'm sorry, Lieutenant Hendrix, but your orders have been changed," she said. This woman never seemed to bring good news.

"Which Lieutenant Hendrix are you talking to?" I asked angrily.

Pointing to Patti she said, "That one. We are not up to sufficient strength in our nursing personnel to allow her to leave. I have spoken to corps headquarters in Saigon. She is staying here."

We were both dumbfounded. How could this happen to us after all we had been through together?

I swore aloud that I was not going to leave without her. I would rather lose my leg than leave Patti behind, but I had no choice.

The supervisor took Patti's arm and gently led her away.

The transport shut its doors and taxied to the runway. I was lying next to a small window. As we took off, I could see Patti waving goodbye.

Silently, I began to weep. For a second, and only a second, I was pleased. After all I had seen and done, I realized I was still capable of the simplest of all human emotion.

Through my scratched and foggy window, I saw my life slowly turn and walk away.

Another tear streaked down my face. Many more followed. My heart was broken.

It is a moment that will stay in my mind forever.

# Chapter 9

M y route home was much the same as it had been when
I had been wounded during my first tour of duty in
Vietnam two years before.
It took weeks going from one hospital to another. Vietnam, Japan, Hawaii, then finally the United States.
The difference was that, before, I had left nothing behind.
This time I left behind my soul.
Patti.
She meant everything to me. Without her I knew I would never be whole.
Weeks later I and many others, too many others, arrived home aboard a medical transport at McChord Air Force Base in Tacoma, Washington. The more seriously wounded were taken off the aircraft first while I waited my turn from my stretcher.
Later, I noticed a familiar face breeze by.
Taking a chance, I called out, "Hey, Air Force!"
The person I had recognized turned toward me and, clutching a large, seemingly heavy green bag, stopped dead in his tracks.
Smiling, he looked at me.

"Well, if it isn't Army! If I'd known you were aboard I would have smuggled you some real food. That plastic tube going to your arm doesn't look like a taste treat."

"If I'd known you were the pilot of this bucket, I would have called my travel agent for a refund," I answered quietly.

"Where's that wife of yours?" he asked. "She must be around here somewhere."

"What's in the bag?" I asked. "Anything in there I'd be familiar with? It seems like you're in a hurry."

With a wink, a smile, and a wave he was gone.

Moments later I was put on a bus, processed and, along with the many others, transferred to Madigan Army Medical Center.

My mother, of course, knew that I had been wounded again.

When I arrived at Madigan, Mom was waiting.

"Lieutenant Hendrix, welcome back to Ward 9A," the chief nurse said. "Considering the amount of time you've spend here in the past, we've had your old bed bronzed."

"Thanks for caring," I answered.

My mother, standing nearby, did not appreciate our humor.

"Are you OK?" she asked.

"I'm fine," I answered.

"No, you're not," she said.

"Yes, I am!" I answered, surprised.

"You can't be. Patti has written ten letters. She telephoned three times. She waited hours to get a turn to call each time. You've never answered a letter or a call. Why?"

"Did you come here to welcome me home or give me a lesson in life?" I asked.

"Both," she said. "You'll recover from your wounds. There's another larger problem. You are breaking both your heart and Patti's. Can't you feel it?"

"Yes, mother. It's true. I love Patti but I don't think I'm good enough for her. In my own way, I've tried to give her the opportunity to change her mind. She can do better," I said.

I finally expressed in words what I now knew had been silently eating at my gut.

I was worried that Patti wouldn't feel the same about me in a normal world. Could she accept me as a husband who went to work at 9 A.M. and came home just after 5 P.M.?

Patti was both brilliant and beautiful! She could have anyone she wanted at home. Why would she want to keep me?

Mother spoke quietly saying the words I needed to hear, "Because she loves you. Just like I do."

"Now, my son, how's your leg?" she asked as her fingers gently touched my right foot and, by feel, counted my toes under my bed sheets. Finding five, she smiled.

The next morning Mother sat on a chair near the foot of my bed. She filled me in on all the latest family happenings.

Just before doctors rounds she had to leave. She kissed my cheek and pressed a pile of letters to my palm.

They were all from Patti. They had been following me as I was transferred from hospital to hospital during my journey home.

I read them slowly, one by one, over and over.

About an hour later I received a telephone call.

Wonder of wonders. It was Patti.

It was 2 A.M. in Vietnam.

"Why haven't you written?" she asked.

"I was afraid you wouldn't love me in the real world. It'll be different here. I may lose my leg. You can do so much better than me."

"You are my life," she said. "One leg or two, or no legs, I love you. Someday soon I'll be with you and I'll be able to prove it to you. I know you're concerned about all that's happened. Please write. We mean too much to each other. We are soul mates."

My fear had not been my loss of love for her but what might be her loss of love for me. Now I knew that I had been wrong even to consider that possibility.

I wrote Patti every day thereafter.

I also wrote my senator, my congressman, the President of the United States, and anyone else who would listen and might be in a position to bring Patti home.

What had been my confusion concerning our love now became my mission fueled by a heart rendering passion of true love. I would do whatever it would take to bring Patti home and be at my side.

Finally I received a letter from my congressman. He wrote that considering all that Patti had done for our country, it was time she came home.

That same day, I was told I would keep my leg. By then I had healed enough to graduate to crutches. It made it easier for me to get to the telephone and call those who had helped bring Patti home and say thank you.

Soon after receiving the letter from my congressman, I was ordered to report to the commander of the hospital where I was a patient.

"Sir, Lieutenant Hendrix reporting, sir!" I stated as I entered his office.

"Lieutenant," he said, "you are a pain in my fanny. Stop writing letters and telephoning everyone in Washington, D.C. Call off the dogs. Now. Your wife will be transferred to a staff position at this hospital very soon. I believe she is already on her way here."

"Lieutenant," he asked quickly, cutting me off from my thanking him, "is it true that you had considered a military career?"

"Yes, sir," I answered.

"Forget it. I don't like politicians or people under my command who play politics," he said. "Your promotion to captain is denied. Upon your release from this hospital, you will be discharged from the US Army. Your discharge will be 'honorable' as there is no law saying you couldn't do as you seem to have done. However, we don't want people in this organization who will not follow proper channels."

My heart pounded in my chest. "I tried proper channels, sir," I said, "but they don't work. I was trained to respect authority. However, since I've been out of combat, I've not found the authority to respect. When the army couldn't assist us, I engaged the target any way I could to accomplish what I believed needed to be done."

"You are dismissed, lieutenant!"

"With pleasure, sir," I answered.

The next day Patti was to return to American soil.

I awaited Patti's arrival in the passenger lounge at the nearby Air Force base. Her transport landed only a few hours late from its scheduled arrival.

I looked everywhere for Patti. She was nowhere to be found.

Later, after waiting for the next transport and not finding her, I sadly, silently, gave the flowers I had brought for Patti to an enlisted man who had just arrived home from Vietnam. I had noticed that he was waiting for his wife and the new child he had met for the first time to drive over from the parking lot and pick him up.

I turned to leave the reception area. I was fighting the doors to the exit with my new crutches when, behind me, I heard someone shout, "Hey, Army!"

There, through my damp blurry eyes, I saw a vision.

I saw Patti.

Behind her stood my Air Force pilot friend to whom, months before, I had traded all my "stuff" for a ride to Phu Bai and Patti's unit.

It is indeed a small world.

"Special delivery, Army," he said. "She missed her flight out of Japan. I saw her in the terminal. It just so happened I was headed this direction with another load of wounded. She explained what happened so I brought her along."

"Well," he said, "gotta go. Bye."

To this day I do not believe I ever heard his real name. He never wore his required regulation uniform name tag. "Air Force" always seemed to work very well.

Patti and I stood and stared at each other for what seemed like hours before falling into each other's arms.

✦ ✦ ✦

Today, twenty-eight years later, my love for Patti has only grown stronger. If it's possible, I love her even more than that first day I saw her.

Since then, Patti has given me three beautiful daughters: Heather, Heidi, and Hollyann. Our love for each other was the little good that came out of the Vietnam War. In that, our children are true examples of that love.

Each day I remind myself of those vows we spoke to each other so many years ago in a place so far away: "To have and to hold each other, forever." Just the beginning . . .